The
Holy Spirit

The Holy Spirit

A Biblical Study

Jack Cottrell

College Press Publishing Company
Joplin, Missouri

Toll-free order line 800-289-3300
On the web at www.collegepress.com

Unless otherwise noted, all scripture references are taken from the
NEW AMERICAN STANDARD BIBLE®, © Copyright 1960, 1962,
1963, 1968, 1971, 1972, 1973, 1975, 1977, 1995 by
The Lockman Foundation. Used by permission.
www.Lockman.org

Cover design by Brett Lyerla

Library of Congress Cataloging-in-Publication Data

Cottrell, Jack.
  The Holy Spirit: a biblical study / by Jack Cottrell.
      p. cm.
  ISBN 0-89900-511-X (softback)
 1. Holy Spirit—Biblical teaching. I. Title.
  BS680.H56C68 2006
  231'.3—dc22

                    2006001793

TABLE
OF
CONTENTS

We proclaim Him,
admonishing every man
and teaching every man
with all wisdom,
so that we may present every man
complete in Christ.
For this purpose also I labor,
striving **according to His power,
which mightily works within me**.

Colossians 1:28-29, NASB

≈ 1 ≈
WHO IS
THE HOLY SPIRIT?

We read much in the Bible about the Holy Spirit, beginning in Genesis 1:2, which speaks of "the Spirit of God." We pray about the Spirit: "May the Spirit guide us." We sing of the Spirit: "Praise Father, Son, and Holy Ghost." Or, "Open my eyes, illumine me, Spirit divine." Or, "Spirit of the living God, fall afresh on me." Someone may ask us, "Have you been filled—or baptized—with the Spirit?"

Exactly what is the "Holy Spirit"? This first lesson seeks to answer this question; it is a study of the *person* of the Holy Spirit. When we analyze the Bible's teaching about Jesus Christ, we usually divide it into two main subjects: the person of Christ (Who is he?) and the work of Christ (What has he done for us?). We do the same with the Bible's teaching on the Holy Spirit. This chapter deals with the *person* of the Spirit; the rest of this book will discuss the Spirit's *work*.

Who is the Holy Spirit? The bottom-line answer is that the Holy Spirit is a *divine person*, generally referred to as the third person of the Trinity (as distinct from the first and second persons, the Father and the Son). This is the mainstream, orthodox Christian view.

> The Holy Spirit is a *divine person.*

Not everyone within the broad scope of Christendom has accepted this understanding, though. As early as the third century A.D. a unitarian view of God called *modalism* was proposed. This is the idea that God is only one person, but he reveals himself in three ways or "modes," one of which is the "Holy Spirit." The Spirit is thus divine and personal, but is the same person as the "Father" and the "Son." Modern unitarianism arose as Socinianism in the six-teenth century and continues today in various forms, most of which are radically humanistic or at best pantheistic. In such contexts the Spirit of God is usually not thought of as a person at all.

The traditional doctrine of the Holy Spirit is also denied by certain modern cults, which typically take biblical references to the Spirit as meaning God's power or "active force." For example, the Jehovah's Witnesses' *New World Translation* of the Bible never capitalizes "holy spirit"; e.g., on Pentecost the disciples "became filled with holy spirit" (Acts 2:4). A Jehovah's Witness author explains, "Were they 'filled' with a person? No, but they were filled with God's active force" (*The Truth That Leads to Eternal Life*, 24). For another example, a spokesman for Herbert W. Armstrong's original, unreformed Worldwide Church of God said, "The Holy Spirit is not a person but the power God the Father uses—much as a man uses electricity" (*Tomorrow's World*, Sept./Oct. 1970, 32). Victor Paul Wierwille's group, The Way International, has a similar view of the Holy Spirit.

Contrary to such antibiblical and antitrinitarian teaching, we will show first that the Holy Spirit is a *person*, and then that he is a *divine* person.

The Holy Spirit Is a Person

The Holy Spirit is a person in the fullest sense of the word. We may think of a "person" as a being who has rational consciousness, self-consciousness, self-determination, and relationships with other persons (Cottrell, *God the Creator*, 235-237). Such characteristics are possessed by each of the three persons of the Trinity, including the Holy Spirit. This is supported by the following biblical data.

The Concept of "Spirit"

The biblical words for "spirit" can be used for things of no substance at all, such as air in motion (wind, John 3:8; breath,

2 Thess 2:8) or attitudes (Eph 4:23; 2 Tim 1:7). However, when substantive beings or entities are called
"spirits," they are always persons. The very concept of
"spirit" denotes personhood. All spiritual beings are
personal beings.

> All spiritual beings are personal beings.

This is true of human beings, who are composed (in part) of
spirit (Acts 7:59; Heb 12:23). It is true also of angelic beings,
both good angels (Heb 1:14) and fallen angels (Matt 12:43,45).
And it is true of God as such: "God is spirit" (John 4:24). Human
beings, angelic beings, and the divine being are all spirit (*pneuma*), and all are *personal* beings. There is no such thing as an
impersonal *being*.

The very fact that the Bible's consistent name for the third person of the Trinity is "Spirit" or "Holy Spirit" is a testimony to the
fact of his personal nature.

The Spirit as *"allos parakletos"*

On the night before his crucifixion, Jesus sought to comfort
his disciples by assuring them that he was not going to abandon
them, leaving them as "orphans" (John 14:18). Though he himself was going to return to heaven, he promised to send to them
the Holy Spirit to take his place: "I will ask the Father, and He
will give you another Helper, that He may be with you forever"
(John 14:16). Jesus specifically identifies this "Helper" as the
Holy Spirit (John 14:26).

The Greek expression for "another Helper" is *allos parakletos.*
This very description underscores the personhood of the Spirit in
two ways. First, the word *parakletos* in itself refers to someone
who is a person. As applied to the Holy Spirit (the "Paraclete"),
this word is translated in various ways: Helper, Counselor,
Comforter, Advocate. The words "Counselor" and "Advocate"
are appropriate because in the first century a *parakletos* was literally a "counselor for the defense," an advocate in the sense of a
defense lawyer. As such, *parakletos* was a personal concept, just as

9

the term "lawyer" is today. The point is that Jesus would not have used this word for the Spirit if the Holy Spirit were not a personal being. Jesus was promising his disciples that the Spirit would come and stand by their sides and be with them and protect them in their future endeavors for his Kingdom.

Second, the word *allos* ("another") in the expresson "another Helper" also points to the Spirit's personhood. The Greek language has two words for "another": *allos* and *heteros*. The latter means "another of a different kind"; *allos* means "another of the

> Jesus promised to send "another Helper" of the same kind as himself.

same kind." It is significant that Jesus used *allos* instead of *heteros*. This means that he promised to send "another Helper" of the same kind as himself. Thus the Spirit must be a personal being, just as Jesus is. As one writer has noted, Jesus' promise would have been of little comfort to the apostles if his promised replacement were something *less* than himself, something less than a person.

Lists of Persons

Another biblical indication of the Spirit's personhood is that he is named and included in lists along with other persons. This includes all the references to the three persons of the Trinity, such as Matt 28:19, "Go therefore and make disciples of all the nations, baptizing them in the name of the Father and the Son and the Holy Spirit." To be paralleled thus with the Father and the Son, who are persons, would make little sense if the Spirit were not also a person. (Other trinitarian passages will be noted below.)

Another reference where the Spirit is paralleled with persons is Acts 15:28, in the letter sent from the apostles and elders and brethren in Jerusalem to Antioch: "For it seemed good to the

> The Spirit as identified in Scripture is paralleled in lists of personal beings.

Holy Spirit and to us to lay upon you no greater burden than these essentials." The writers of the letter are thus saying that the decision in view was made by them *and* by the Spirit. Again, this would not make sense if the Holy Spirit were not a person who can make judgments and decisions, just as the church leaders could.

Pneuma as a Neuter Noun

Another biblical indication of the personhood of the Spirit has to do with Greek grammar. In Greek, for grammatical purposes, every noun has a gender; i.e., it is considered to be either masculine, or feminine, or neuter. When a noun is used in a given context and is accompanied by adjectives or pronouns that refer to that noun, they will have the same gender as the noun. Now, the word for "Spirit," *pneuma*, happens to be neuter. This means that pronouns and other word forms referring to it should also be neuter. This is purely a grammatical device and has nothing to do with the gender, or lack thereof, of the object represented by the noun.

Sometimes a student with a little knowledge of Greek will draw a totally wrong conclusion from this, asserting that since *pneuma* is neuter, the Holy *Pneuma* must be an "it" and not a person at all. As one writer said, "In the original language of the New Testament, which is Greek, the Holy Spirit is consistently 'neuter' as well as the pronouns, articles, and participles which refer to 'It.' In the English translations where a masculine pronoun or noun appears, the original neuter gender has so been changed by a translator." Thus the translators have proceeded to "tamper with the gender of the Godhead" (*Christian Standard*, 10/4/81, 23).

Such comments are quite misguided and are completely misleading because the gender of a *word* (a noun) is not necessarily related to the gender of that for which it stands. E.g., impersonal things that are "neuter" in reality are often represented by words that are masculine or feminine grammatically: *ho artos* (masc.) means "bread," and *he aspis* (fem.) means "shield." At the same time words representing persons may well be neuter: *to andrapodon* refers to a slave or captive in war; *to paidion* means "infant, child." Thus the fact that the word *pneuma* is neuter is totally irrelevant in determining whether the Spirit is a person or not.

11

What *is* relevant, though, is the fact that on a few occasions masculine pronouns are used to refer to the Holy *Pneuma* where we would have expected them to be neuter. Grammatically, they *should* be neuter. But especially in John 16:13-14 and Eph 1:14 the masculine *ekeinos* ("He, that one") and the masculine relative pronoun *hos* ("who") are used instead of neuter forms of these words. This seems to be a deliberate assertion of the Spirit's personhood.

> Biblical use of masculine pronouns in reference to the Holy Spirit affirms the concept of his personhood.

Personal Activities

The most convincing testimony to the personal nature of the Holy Spirit is the fact that he is pictured over and over in the Bible as doing the kinds of things that persons do. He thinks, knows, speaks, decides, teaches, intercedes, testifies, and loves. Consider the following:

1. The Spirit engages in intellectual activity such as thinking and knowing, which is possible only for thinking, rational persons. Romans 8:27 speaks of "the mind of the Spirit." Paul says, "The thoughts of God no one knows except the Spirit of God" (1 Cor 2:11), thus describing the Spirit as a knowing person. In John 14:8 Jesus promises that the coming Spirit will "convict the world concerning sin and righteousness and judgment." The word for "convict" means to demonstrate or to convince via evidence, which is clearly the activity of a reasoning, personal being.

2. The Spirit engages in volitional activity, i.e., using his will to decide, to choose, and to make authoritative decisions. In Acts 13:2 the Spirit indicates that he has chosen Barnabas and Saul for missionary work. In Acts 15:28 the Spirit made a specific judgment or decision ("it seemed good to the Holy Spirit"); in Acts 16:6-7 he is pictured as choosing where Paul and his missionary band should and should not travel. He also decides which Christians will receive which spiritual gifts, "distributing to each one individually just as He wills" (1 Cor 12:11).

> The Holy Spirit does the kinds of things that persons do.

3. The Spirit is often described as speaking, as in the act of revelation: "Whatever He hears, He will speak" (John 16:13). He speaks to Ezekiel (Ezek 2:2; 3:24; 11:5), to Philip (Acts 8:29), to the church at Antioch (Acts 13:2), to Paul (1 Tim 4:1), and to the seven churches in Revelation 2 and 3 (2:7, etc.).

4. The Spirit is depicted as a teacher of men. Addressing the Lord God, Nehemiah 9:20 says, "You gave Your good Spirit to instruct them." Jesus comforted his disciples by promising them that the coming Helper, the Holy Spirit, "will teach you all things" (John 14:26). The inspired Apostle Paul declares that he spoke in words "taught by the Spirit" (1 Cor 2:13).

5. The Spirit experiences emotions or feelings. Romans 15:30 speaks of "the love of the Spirit," which refers to his love for us. He is also capable of grief. In their sin and idolatry against God, the Israelites "rebelled and grieved His Holy Spirit" (Isa 63:10); and Christians are warned, "Do not grieve the Holy Spirit of God" (Eph 4:30). Only persons can experience such emotions as love and grief.

As the object of the actions of others, the Holy Spirit is described as being treated as only a person can be treated. He is lied to (Acts 5:3), tempted (Acts 5:9), blasphemed (Matt 12:31), and insulted (Heb 10:29).

In all of these ways we are presented with a consistent biblical picture of the Holy Spirit as a personal being. Those who deny the Spirit's personhood are simply not taking the biblical testimony seriously.

The Holy Spirit Is a Divine Person

It is not enough to think of the Holy Spirit as a person; we must also remember that he is a *divine* person. He is *God*—God the Holy Spirit, one of the three persons of the Trinity. This means he is equal with the Father and the Son in essence and power

> The Spirit is described as being in a relationship of equality with the Father and the Son.

and in all of his attributes, but he is a distinct person with his own

13

center of consciousness and his own unique activities. The biblical evidence for the Spirit's divinity is as follows.

Trinitarian Texts

One of the main reasons we believe the Holy Spirit is divine is that there are numerous New Testament texts that speak of the Father, the Son, and the Spirit in parallel relationships, indicating equality. The best known is the baptismal formula in Matthew 28:19, "baptizing them in the name of the Father and the Son and the Holy Spirit." In the cultures of Bible days one's name was practically equivalent with the person himself. This text speaks of just one "name" that embraces the three persons equally, indicating shared attributes of deity.

Another trinitarian text is the benediction in 2 Corinthians 13:14, "The grace of the Lord Jesus Christ, and the love of God, and the fellowship of the Holy Spirit, be with you all." Most of the time the Apostle Paul uses the Greek word *theos*, "God," to refer to God the Father; thus again all three persons of the Trinity are paralleled, though not in the same order as Matthew 28:19.

Another text placing the three persons in a relationship of equality is 1 Corinthians 12:4-6: "Now there are varieties of gifts, but the same Spirit. And there are varieties of ministries, and the same Lord. There are varieties of effects, but the same God who works all things in all persons." Since Paul almost always uses the Greek word *kurios*, "Lord," for Jesus Christ, we know that this is another trinitarian text. Here the Holy Spirit appears first, with all three persons of the Trinity being involved in the distribution of spiritual gifts within the church.

Other trinitarian texts include Ephesians 4:4-6, where three of the seven unifying factors for the church are the "one Spirit," the "one Lord," and the "one God and Father of all." In 1 Peter 1:1-2 the three persons of the Trinity are described as contributing thus to our salvation: we are "chosen according to the foreknowledge of God the Father, by the sanctifying work of the

Spirit, to obey Jesus Christ and be sprinkled with His blood." See also 2 Corinthians 1:21-22.

It is also important to note that many passages make it clear that Father, Son, and Spirit are *distinct* persons, i.e., distinct from one another. This is significant because of the false view referred to above "modalism," i.e., the idea that the one and only divine person has chosen to reveal himself progressively in three separate roles or modes. This is totally inconsistent with texts such as Luke 3:21-22, where the Father, Son, and Spirit are each distinctively yet simultaneously involved in the baptism of Jesus. Such a scenario is deceptive and misleading unless the three persons are truly distinct from one another. A similar text is Acts 2:32-33, which says that the risen Jesus was exalted to the right hand of God the Father, who poured forth the Holy Spirit on Pentecost. Unless there are three actual persons involved here, we again face confusion and deception. See also John 14:26; 16:7; Romans 8:11; Ephesians 2:8; Isaiah 48:16.

> The Father, Son, and Spirit are each distinctively yet simultaneously involved in the baptism of Jesus.

Divine Characteristics

Another reason why we believe the Spirit is a *divine* person is that the Bible describes him as having attributes that we associate with deity. For example, Hebrews 9:14 speaks of "the eternal Spirit." Only God has inherent eternality (1 Tim 6:16; Ps 90:2). Also, 1 Corinthians 2:10-11 says that "the Spirit searches all things, even the depths of God," and that he knows the thoughts or things of God. Whoever knows the very thoughts of the omniscient God must himself be omniscient; this is true of the Holy Spirit. Again, Psalm 139:7-10 implies that there is no point in space from which the Spirit is absent; this suggests the divine attribute of omnipresence. The Spirit's involvement in the creation (Gen 1:2; Ps 104:30) and in providence (Zech 4:6) suggests that he also shares in divine omnipotence.

15

Blasphemy against the Spirit

In Matthew 12:31-32 Jesus describes "blasphemy against the Spirit" as a sin that "shall not be forgiven . . . either in this age or in the age to come." As Mark 3:29 puts it, "Whoever blasphemes against the Holy Spirit never has forgiveness, but is guilty of an eternal sin." Blasphemy literally means "speaking against." In this context Jesus is referring to someone who speaks actual words of cursing and denunciation against the Spirit, while at the same time rejecting the Spirit's testimony to Jesus as the Messiah.

What is significant for our purpose here is Jesus' declaration that blasphemy against *himself* (the Son of Man) will be forgiven, but not blasphemy against the Spirit (Matt 12:32; Luke 12:10). Since Jesus is God in the flesh, blasphemy against him is literally blasphemy against God; but such blasphemy can be forgiven if repented of. But in some unexplained way, blasphemy against the Spirit is a worse sin than blasphemy against Jesus, since it allows no forgiveness. This makes no sense whatsoever unless the Holy Spirit is also divine.

The Spirit Is Called God

A final biblical proof of the divinity of the Spirit is the account of Ananias and Sapphira in Acts 5:1-4. Here this married couple is described as selling a piece of property, bringing a part of the proceeds to the apostles as a gift to the church, and then representing the gift as the entire amount received for the property. The Apostle Peter condemns this lie: "Ananias, why has Satan filled your heart to lie to the Holy Spirit . . . ? You have not lied to men but to God."

In these words Peter declares that lying to the Holy Spirit is in reality lying to God himself. This is a clear affirmation that the Spirit is a divine person.

Conclusion

We have seen that there is strong biblical evidence that the Holy Spirit is a divine person. What are some implications of this truth for our Christian practice?

One point is that we should work very hard to train our minds to think of the Spirit in personal terms. This is a bit more difficult than remembering that the Father is a person, since "father" is by nature a personal concept. It is also more difficult than remembering that the Son is a person, since we associate the Son with the person Jesus Christ. Nevertheless we must strive to picture the Spirit who was poured out on Pentecost and who indwells our very bodies as a true and living person. We should never refer to the Spirit as "it." Following the biblical example, we should use personal pronouns such as "he" or "him."

> We should work very hard to train our minds to think of the Spirit in personal terms.

Another point is that our worship of God must include worship of the Holy Spirit. As the "Doxology" says, "Praise Father, Son, and Holy Ghost" (though we otherwise rarely use the King James word "ghost" for referring to the Spirit). We should note, though, that there are no biblical examples or precedents for addressing the Holy Spirit directly in praise or in prayer. The biblical pattern for prayer seems to be that we should pray to the Father (Matt 6:9), in the name of Jesus as mediator (John 14:13-14; 1 Tim 2:5), through the power of the Holy Spirit (Rom 8:26-27).

~2~
THE HOLY SPIRIT
AND THE BIBLE

The three persons of the Trinity are fully equal in their "invisible attributes," in their "eternal power and divine nature" (Rom 1:20). They are each involved in the works of creation and providence. Especially in relation to the work of salvation, however, each person of the Trinity performs works that are mainly or uniquely his own. This is the case with the Holy Spirit, whose works are the subject of the rest of this book.

We may divide the work of the Spirit into two main categories, i.e., he gives us *knowledge* and he gives us *power*. It is crucial that we keep these aspects of his work distinct. In this chapter we are discussing the main way the Spirit gives us knowledge; the remainder of the book is mostly about his gifts of power.

One of the main works of the Holy Spirit is to address our intellects and to provide us with essential knowledge. For Christians throughout the church age and in the world today, the Spirit speaks to our minds through the words of the Bible, God's holy

> **Q: What is the most important thing the Holy Spirit has ever done for us?**
> **A: He gave us the Bible!**

Word. If one were to ask me what I believe is the most important thing the Holy Spirit has ever done for us, I would answer immediately and with conviction: *He gave us the Bible!*

The Holy Spirit and the Origin of the Bible

Our Bible has 66 units or books; each one was originally written by a human author such as Moses, Isaiah, Matthew, or Paul. But what they wrote was not just the product of their own personal experience and speculation. Everything they wrote was produced under the immediate influence of God himself, in the person of the Holy Spirit. In a real sense the Holy Spirit is the author of the Bible; the Bible is his gift to us.

Revelation and Inspiration

Traditionally Christians have described the Bible as *revealed* and *inspired*. Both of these works are involved in God's communication with us. On a human level communication is the process of transferring a thought or concept from one person's mind to the mind of another. We can do this through such means as facial expressions, gestures, or words. This is not as easy as it might seem at first. We can think of all kinds of scenarios where this communication is crucial, such as being warned by someone about a potential danger or being directed by a doctor through a prescribed treatment program. Unfortunately, though, human communication is often hindered or corrupted by such things as faulty memories, incomplete understanding, and poor choice of words. We are, after all, finite creatures; and our powers of communication are finite.

One of the most wondrous of marvels is the fact that the Creator of the universe, God himself, has determined to communicate with us, his creatures! He desires to share his very thoughts with us! This is an awesome concept in itself, but given our sinful situation it becomes a matter of eternal consequence. Among other things, God must communicate with us to tell us how to be saved from our sin. This is in part the very purpose of the Bible.

> The Holy Spirit gives knowledge and power to God's people.

In view of our desperate need to hear God's message to us, in view of God's choice to use human spokesmen to deliver this message, and in view of the potential problems involved in the communication process, how did God ensure that what the biblical writers documented for us is what he himself wanted us to hear?

This is where the Spirit's work of revelation and inspiration enters the picture. The purpose of revelation and inspiration is to make sure that the Bible contains all the information we need for godliness and salvation, and that it is communicated to us in a form that is complete and free from error.

A large part of the biblical material was revealed directly to its human authors by the power of the Holy Spirit. This is true of anything in Scripture that could not have been known by any human being, such as the account of creation in Genesis 1. It is also true of any prophecy of a future event planned or foreknown by God, such as Isaiah 53. Such material could be known only through revelation. On the other hand, other parts of the Bible are not the result of revelation but were known to the writers from their own experiences, such as Acts 21:1-16 (note Luke's "we") and Romans 16:1-23 (Paul's personal greetings). Some parts may be a combination of both divine revelation and human sentiments (e.g., the Psalms). In any case, the revealed elements originate from the Holy Spirit.

But a question still remains. Why should we trust and obey *any* part of the Bible, even its revealed parts, given that every bit of it has been mediated to us through finite human authors who are subject to errors in the communication process? Here is where the Spirit's work of *inspiration* becomes crucial. When the Bible writers were preparing the original written texts of their messages, the Holy Spirit was working within them not only to reveal some things to them but also to make sure that *whatever* they wrote was absolutely true and without error. Whatever influence was necessary to bring about this result is what we call "the inspiration of the Holy Spirit." While not all the Bible is revealed, it is all *inspired*; and in the final analysis inspiration is the reason why all Scripture is completely trustworthy and authoritative.

> Q: Why should we trust and obey any part of the Bible? A: Because of the Holy Spirit's work of inspiration in the totality of Scripture.

Biblical Testimony to the Spirit's Role

The Bible itself gives us abundant testimony to the Spirit's role in its own origin. David, who wrote many of the Psalms, says,

21

"The Spirit of the Lord spoke by me, and His word was on my tongue" (2 Sam 23:2). Citing Psalm 110:1, Jesus says that David wrote these words "in the Holy Spirit" (Mark 12:36). Citing another Psalm, the Apostle Peter says in Acts 1:16 that "the Scripture had to be fulfilled, which the Holy Spirit foretold by the mouth of David." Citing Psalm 2:1-2, Acts 4:24-26 says that these words were spoken "by the Holy Spirit through the mouth of our father David." Citing a passage from Isaiah, the Apostle Paul declares that "the Holy Spirit rightly spoke [it] through Isaiah the prophet" (Acts 28:25-27). See also Hebrews 3:7-11; 9:8; 10:15; 1 Peter 1:10-11.

The role of the Spirit in bringing about the Old Testament writings ("the prophetic word," 2 Pet 1:19) is especially emphasized by the Apostle Peter in 2 Peter 1:20-21: "Above all, you must understand that no prophecy of Scripture came about by the prophet's own interpretation. For prophecy never had its origin in the will of man, but men spoke from God as they were carried along by the Holy Spirit" (NIV). This translation makes it clear that Peter is speaking here of the *origin* of the Bible, not some reader's interpretation of it. That is, no part of the prophetic Word came into existence merely by some human being sitting down and declaring, "I think I'll write a book of the Bible!" No, whatever the role of the human author, the ultimate cause and source for the biblical writings is clearly the Holy Spirit: "Men spoke from God as they were carried along by the Holy Spirit."

> "Men spoke from God as they were carried along by the Holy Spirit."

When Jesus promised to send "another Helper" to his Apostles after he returned to heaven (John 14:16), he told them that one of the Spirit's main purposes in their lives would be to ensure that they would always speak truth when teaching about Jesus. See John 14:26: "But the Helper, the Holy Spirit, whom the Father will send in My name, He will teach you all things, and bring to your remembrance all that I said to you." Here Jesus says the Spirit will help the Apostles in two ways. One, he will give them infallible memories of everything they had heard Jesus teach during his earthly ministry; this is part of what is involved in inspiration. Two, "He will teach you all things," i.e., he will reveal new things to them. See John 15:26.

Jesus adds to this promise in John 16:12-14: "I have many more things to say to you, but you cannot bear them now. But when He, the Spirit of truth, comes, He will guide you into all the truth; for He will not speak on His own initiative, but whatever He hears, He will speak; and He will disclose to you what is to come. He will glorify Me, for He will take of Mine and will disclose it to you." This is a clear promise of new revelation that would be given to the Apostles by the "Spirit of truth." The Spirit's inspiring work is implied in the assurance that what they taught would be *truth*. This promise applies to the Apostles' preaching and oral teaching, and also to their writings.

The same would apply to any nonapostle upon whom the Spirit bestowed the gift of prophecy. The teaching of the inspired Apostles and (New Testament) Prophets in one sense forms the very foundation upon which the church is built (Eph 2:20; 3:5).

The Apostle Paul was conscious of the fact that the Holy Spirit was working within him (via revelation and inspiration) as he was writing his New Testament letters. "I think that I also have the Spirit of God," he declares (1 Cor 7:40). He speaks of God's wonderful mysteries and declares, "For to us God revealed them through the Spirit" (1 Cor 2:10). He says that he knows he has received "the Spirit who is from God, so that we may know the things freely given to us by God, which things we also speak, not in words taught by human wisdom, but in those taught by the Spirit, combining spiritual thoughts with spiritual words" (1 Cor 2:12-13). The latter is a clear reference to the Spirit's role in guarding the very words which he spoke or wrote. See Eph 3:5; 1 Tim 4:1.

The Importance of Inspiration

Some Christians get a bit nervous when the subject of biblical inspiration is raised because they mistakenly assume that inspiration means that the Holy Spirit must have *dictated* every word of Scripture to its human authors. This is clearly not the case, as the above discussion shows. The key distinction is between *revelation* and *inspiration*.

The fact is that the Spirit performed these functions in different ways. As Hebrews 1:1 says, God "spoke long ago to the fathers in the prophets in many portions and in many ways." In some circumstances inspiration may have involved a kind of dictated revelation, but this was certainly not necessary in most cases. At the other end of the spectrum we may picture the Spirit as *supervising* the experience-based writings of human authors. As the latter wrote, the Spirit would simply watch for any imminent problems and would then intervene in the thinking and writing process only where necessary to guard against error or incompleteness.

> We may picture the Spirit as supervising the experience-based writings of human authors.

The real issue regarding the Spirit's inspiration of Scripture is not the process, but the product or result of it. The result is no less than this, that the Bible is the very Word of God, indeed, the very *words* of God. In Romans 3:2 Paul describes the Old Testament writings as "the oracles of God," or more specifically, "the very words of God" (NIV). Paul knew that when he taught under the inspiration of the Spirit, his message was not "the word of men" but "the word of God" (1 Thess 2:13). Because it *is* the Word of God, "the Scripture cannot be broken," as Jesus says (John 10:35). It is *truth* (John 17:17).

> The Bible is the very Word of God, indeed, the very *words* of God.

Thus when we hold a Bible, insofar as it accurately represents the original text penned by Apostles and Prophets, we have in our very hands a permanent, errorless record of God's will for us and God's message of hope to us. Nothing the Spirit could do for us is more vital than this. No wonder we can say that the most important thing the Holy Spirit ever did for us is to give us the Bible!

The Holy Spirit and the Understanding of the Bible

Orthodox Christianity has always believed that the Holy Spirit had a unique role in the *origin* of Scripture. Not as widely accepted is the belief that the Spirit also has a specific role in the *understanding* of the Bible. This latter belief is called the doctrine of *illumination*. It says that the Spirit works directly upon believers' minds as we study Scripture, giving us definitive, subjective help in understanding its meaning.

> The Spirit speaks to our minds through the words of the Bible.

Illumination Defended

Those who accept this doctrine of illumination say that it is specifically taught in certain biblical passages. They say that these texts are intended to apply to all Christians and are God's promise that the Spirit will lead us to a true understanding of the Bible.

Texts cited as proof of this doctrine begin with John 14:26, which says that the Holy Spirit "will teach you all things, and bring to your remembrance all that I said to you"; and John 16:13, which promises that "the Spirit of truth . . . will guide you into all the truth." Also cited is 1 Corinthians 2:10-16, which says that the Spirit "searches . . . the depths of God," and is given to us "that we may know the things freely given to us by God." Referring to this passage, R.C. Sproul says, "*Illumination* concerns the Spirit's work in assisting the reader to achieve clarity in understanding the content of the Word. It is the Spirit who 'searches' the deep things of God and works to assist our naturally carnal minds to understand spiritual things (1 Cor. 2:10,14)."[1]

Another commonly cited text is 1 John 2:20,27, "But You have an anointing from the Holy One, and you all know. . . . As for you, the anointing which you received from Him abides in you, and you have no need for anyone to teach you; but as His anointing teaches you about all things, and is true and is not a lie,

25

and just as it has taught you, you abide in Him." This "anointing" is said to be the Holy Spirit, who dwells in us to teach us all things. Other texts cited in defense of this doctrine are Matthew 10:19-20 and Jeremiah 31:31-34.

Crucial to the doctrine of illumination is the assumption that the key texts noted above refer not just to the apostles but to all Christians. As one writer said in a letter to *Christian Standard* (5/1/94, 23), "The same Holy Spirit that told holy men of old what to write in the Bible also indwells Christians today and continues to prompt, lead, and speak to us," as promised in 1 Corinthians 2:12-13 and John 16:13. R.A. Torrey, declaring that "the Holy Spirit will teach us all things," says that John 16:12-14 "is the privilege of each believer in Jesus Christ, even the humblest." Torrey says, "We shall never truly know the truth until we are thus taught directly by the Holy Spirit."[2]

This doctrine is reflected in traditional hymns. "Open My Eyes" includes these lines: "Open my eyes that I may see glimpses of truth thou hast for me. . . . Open my eyes, illumine me, Spirit divine." The song "Break Thou the Bread of Life" says, "Oh send Thy Spirit, Lord, now unto me, that He may touch my eyes and make me see. Show me the truth concealed within Thy word, and in Thy book revealed I see the Lord."

We should note that the concept of illumination is rooted in the Augustinian doctrine of total depravity, as found today especially in Calvinism (though many non-Augustinians have adopted it also). The Calvinist Edwin Palmer says that the unsaved man "is blind, blind as a mole, so that he cannot see the great and clear truths even when they are presented to him by an apostle. . . . He cannot see a thing. . . . A veil has covered his heart. His eyes are closed." But then comes the Holy Spirit, who "gives man not only an infallible book, but also eyes so that he can read that book." The Spirit "enlightens man . . . by mysteriously operating on his heart so he can see the revelation already given."[3]

Within this context the starting point for the Spirit's ongoing illumination is the conversion experience, brought about by the Spirit's gift of irresistible grace.

Illumination Refuted

In my judgment the concept of illumination is a false doctrine. The Bible does not teach that the Holy Spirit is given to Christian believers for the purpose of giving us knowledge. The only *knowledge* provided for the church today as a specific work of the Holy Spirit is the knowledge that comes to us through the Bible, not through any kind of direct working upon an individual's mind or intellect.

I have three basic reasons for denying the doctrine of illumination. One, Christian people who claim to be illuminated by the Spirit often have different and even opposite understandings of the same passage or teaching of Scripture. Examples are texts dealing with gender roles, texts dealing with the end times and the millennium, and texts dealing with God's sovereignty and man's free will. If the Spirit is leading all Christians into a true understanding of the Bible, why do we not have unity in our understanding? Indeed, why do we not all believe that illumination is a true doctrine?

Two, in the final analysis illumination is a useless idea, for even those who believe in it recognize that individual Christians grow in their understanding and sometimes change their interpretations of Scripture. For example, Palmer says, "We still have considerable dimness in our eyes (some more than others); we still are not free from blindness; we still cannot see as well as we should. So we should pray constantly as Christians that the Spirit of wisdom and revelation will come and illuminate our minds so that we may see more of the great truths of revelation."[4] Does this mean that every time I change my mind about a biblical teaching, I must assume that my former belief was erroneous and that the Spirit has now shown me the truth? But how can I know that my present belief about anything is my final one, and that the Spirit will not "correct" me in the future? Of what practical value, then, is this doctrine?

Three, the doctrine of illumination must be rejected because there is no real exegetical basis for it. For one thing, its theological basis—total depravity—is itself a false doctrine (Cottrell, *The Faith Once for All*, 197-200). Most significantly, the key texts used to support it (John 14:26; 16:13; 1 Cor 2:10-16) apply only to the Spirit's work of revelation and inspiration with reference to apostles and prophets. They are not general promises to all Christians; to apply them thus is a serious error.

But what about 1 John 2:20,27? What about the "anointing" that all have received, and that teaches us all things? This cannot be a reference to the Holy Spirit. Even if it were, these verses would not teach illumination but would teach that the Spirit has directly revealed all truth to each Christian. This would make the Bible itself unnecessary; it would make Christian teachers unnecessary; it would also produce unanimity of understanding of the things of God among believers. But none of these things is true. Thus we must deny that these verses teach illumination.

The best interpretation of 1 John 2:20,27 is that the "anointing" refers to the *Word of God* itself, as originally taught by inspired apostles and prophets and as possessed by all Christians in the form of the Bible. The "Holy One" who gives us this anointing is himself the Holy Spirit (v. 20). This anointing abides in us (v. 27); in this context the Word of God is said to abide in us (vv. 14,24); see also 2 John 2; John 5:38; 15:7; Colossians 3:16. This anointing "is true and is not a lie" (v. 27); this description applies more to the teaching than to the teacher himself.

Though we must reject the doctrine of illumination as such, this does not mean that God gives us no help in understanding the Bible. We can expect such help, but *not* as some unique work of the Holy Spirit. It is part of God's special providential intervention in answer to prayer (see the prayers in Eph 1:17-18; Phil 1:9-10; Col 1:9; Ps 119:18). The answers to such prayers may be the work of the Father, or of the Son, or of the Spirit.

Such help in understanding the Bible may come through the gift of *wisdom*, in answer to the prayer mandated in James 1:5. This will not be new knowledge, but discernment in how to use and apply what is already known in Scripture.

Such help may also come through providentially sent human teachers. On the need for human teachers, see Acts 8:30-31; 1 Corinthians 12:28; Ephesians 4:11; Hebrews 5:11–6:3. If illumination were a fact, no human teachers would be needed.

God may also providentially aid us in understanding the Bible in various other ways, such as sharpening our mental processes, clearing our preoccupied minds, preventing distractions, helping us to concentrate, and helping us to recall ideas and to put them together.

The Holy Spirit's specific work of sanctification may indirectly help us to understand Scripture, since one of the greatest hindrances to true understanding is the sinful, rebellious will. That is, we often willfully misinterpret Scripture because we do not want to conform our lives to its true meaning. The whole point of sanctification is to soften our rebellious wills, which often clears the way for acknowledging the true meaning of the Bible.

NOTES

1. R.C. Sproul, "The Internal Testimony of the Holy Spirit," in *Inerrancy,* ed. by Norman Geisler (Grand Rapids: Zondervan, 1979), 337.

2. R.A. Torrey, *The Person and Work of the Holy Spirit* (New York: Revell, 1910), 143-144.

3. Edwin Palmer, *The Person and Ministry of the Holy Spirit* (Grand Rapids: Baker, 1974), 54-59.

4. Ibid., 61.

3

THE HOLY SPIRIT AND THE NEW AGE

From this point on we will be dealing with the work of the Holy Spirit in terms of the *power* that he bestows upon his people. Holy Spirit power falls into three general categories: miraculous power, which is the power to work miracles or do other obviously supernatural things; ministering power, which is the ability to perform works of service for the body of believers; and moral power, which is a strengthening of the will to enable obedience to the Lord's commands. The first two often overlap.

World history is divided into two major periods: the age *before* the first coming of Jesus Christ (B.C.), and the age *after* his coming (A.D.). For calendar purposes the specific transition point is the birth of Jesus. However, in terms of the conditions under which God deals with his people, the transition is actually the death of Jesus. This refers to the change from the Old Covenant era to the New Covenant era. When Jesus died on the cross, the Old Covenant age came to an end, and the New Covenant age began. For specific purposes related to Christ's resurrection and ascension, this new age was not formally inaugurated until the Day of Pentecost, as recorded in Acts 2.

> When Jesus died on the cross, the Old Covenant age came to an end, and the New Covenant age began.

Thus in a real sense Pentecost was the beginning of a truly *new age*, an age that continues to this very day. One thing that makes it *new* is the role played by the Holy Spirit in this age. The significance of Pentecost is that it was the beginning of a *new* work of the Spirit. Our purpose here is to see Pentecost in this light.

Prophecies and Promises
of a New Age of the Holy Spirit

The Spirit was present and working throughout the Old
Testament era. At the time of creation, "the Spirit of God was
moving over the surface of the waters" (Gen 1:2). In preflood
days the Spirit of God was actively striving in unspecified ways to
stem the increasing sinfulness of the race (Gen 6:3). During the
history of Israel many prophets spoke to God's people through
the power of the Spirit (2 Sam 23:2; 2 Pet 2:20-21). The Spirit
came upon many of Israel's leaders, equipping them with wisdom
and ministry skills. For example, the Spirit was upon Moses (Num
11:17). Craftsmen such as Bezalel and Oholiab were filled with
the Spirit of God, to equip them with the skills necessary for
building the tabernacle (Exod 31:1-5). "The Spirit of the LORD
came upon Gideon" (Judg 6:34). The Spirit came
upon Samson "mightily" (Judg 14:6,19), as he did
also upon King Saul (1 Sam 10:10). Likewise,
when Samuel anointed the shepherd boy David,
"the Spirit of the LORD came mightily upon David from that day
forward" (1 Sam 16:13). These are examples of the reality of the
Spirit's work in the "old age."

> **The Holy Spirit was present and working throughout the Old Testament.**

But in this Old Testament era there are significant prophecies
of a future age that would be marked by a *new* and *special* presence of the Spirit. Isaiah 44:3 says, "For I will pour out water on
the thirsty land and streams on the dry ground; I will pour out My
Spirit on your offspring and My blessing on your descendants"
(see Isa 32:15). Ezekiel 36:25-27 prophesies, "Then I will sprin-
kle clean water on you, and you will be clean; I will cleanse you
from all your filthiness and from all your idols. Moreover, I will
give you a new heart and put a new spirit within you; and I will
remove the heart of stone from your flesh and give you a heart of
flesh. I will put My Spirit within you and cause you to walk in My
statutes, and you will be careful to observe My ordinances." Most
significant is Joel 2:28-29: "It will come about after this that I will

pour out My Spirit on all mankind; and your sons and daughters will prophesy, your old men will dream dreams, your young men will see visions. Even on the male and female servants I will pour out My Spirit in those days."

Such promises of the coming age of the Spirit are found also in the Gospels. Though these promises are recorded in the New Testament Scriptures, they preceded the Pentecost event and thus are simply continuing the prophetic theme begun by Isaiah, Ezekiel, and Joel. As foretold by John the Baptist, "As for me, I baptize you with water for repentance, but He who is coming after me is mightier than I . . . ; He will baptize you with the Holy Spirit and fire" (Matt 3:11; see Mark 1:7-8; Luke 3:16; John 1:33). In Luke 11:13 Jesus says, "If you then, being evil, know how to give good gifts to your children, how much more will your heavenly Father give the Holy Spirit to those who ask Him?" Most significant is an event recorded in John 7:37-39:

> Now on the last day, the great day of the feast, Jesus stood and cried out, saying, "If anyone is thirsty, let him come to Me and drink. He who believes in Me, as the Scripture said, 'From his innermost being will flow rivers of living water.'" But this He spoke of the Spirit, whom those who believed in Him were to receive; for the Spirit was not yet given, because Jesus was not yet glorified.

See John 4:7-14.

Just before his ascension Jesus renewed this promise, this time in the words of John the Baptist. Jesus told his apostles to wait in Jerusalem for the imminent arrival of "what the Father had promised . . . 'for John baptized with water, but you will be baptized with the Holy Spirit not many days from now'" (Acts 1:4-5). He adds, "You will receive power when the Holy Spirit has come upon you" (Acts 1:8).

At this point I will make three comments about this crescendo of prophecies and promises. First, all these passages refer to the coming of the Holy Spirit in terms of *water*. The Spirit will be "poured out"; people will be "baptized with the Holy Spirit"; those who believe

> The coming of the Holy Spirit is described in terms of water.

33

will "drink" the Spirit and thus ingest "living water." The obvious point is the connection between water and life; the Spirit will be a source of inner, spiritual life. The different water analogies depicting *how* the Holy Spirit is received (by being poured out, by being baptized with, by drinking) are completely incidental and all refer to the same event in the Christian's life. The figure of baptism with the Spirit was suggested to John by his own work of baptizing in water. The figure of drinking the Spirit was appropriate for Jesus to use under the circumstances both of John 4 (drawing water from a well) and of John 7 (a water ceremony during the Feast of Tabernacles). Both figures are used in 1 Corinthians 12:13, which says that all Christians have been baptized "by one Spirit," and "we were all made to drink of one Spirit." These are just two ways of referring to the same event.

My second comment is that all of these pre-Pentecostal prophecies and promises are pointing ahead to something that will be *new* and *different*, compared to the way the Spirit was working in the Old Covenant era itself. This new work of the Spirit will not be just a repeat of what was already happening, nor will it be just a quantitative increase in the number of people who would be recipients thereof. The new-age working of the Spirit would be something qualitatively new.

Third, in view of the emphatic nature of these prophecies, this new-age blessing of the Spirit would be something truly grand and wonderful, something that stands out as characteristic of the New Testament age. Indeed, it would be one of the unique and distinguishing elements of this new age, namely the gift and indwelling presence of the *Holy Spirit* in the heart and body of every Christian.

> One of the unique and distinguishing elements of this new age is the gift and indwelling presence of the Holy Spirit in the heart and body of every Christian.

Pentecostal Miracles

All agree that the prophecies discussed above were fulfilled on the Day of Pentecost, as recorded in the second chapter of Acts.

This was the beginning of the age of "the baptism in the Holy Spirit." There is much disagreement, however, as to the *meaning* of Pentecost (and therefore as to the meaning of "baptism in the Spirit"). Some say that all the prophecies and promises of the Spirit were pointing specifically to the *miraculous* events of Pentecost, and that the *new* thing was the miraculous power manifested there, especially in the speaking of tongues.

This view is common in the Restoration Movement, especially as an interpretation of the phrase, "baptism in the Holy Spirit." Such "baptism in the Spirit" is said to be the empowerment to speak in tongues and perhaps to perform other miracles. But those who hold this view usually limit the fulfillment of this promise to two events only: Pentecost itself, and the conversion of Cornelius. The former is the main performance; the latter is the one encore.

Pentecostals and Charismatics agree that the purpose of "baptism in the Spirit" is to bestow the gift of tongues and other miraculous gifts. Their view, however is that these miraculous gifts are meant for all believers throughout the Christian era.

Another view, the one defended here, is that the main point of the coming of the Holy Spirit on Pentecost was *not* miracles such as tongues, but the *indwelling gift and sanctifying presence* of the Spirit in believers.

Why do we say that the main point of Pentecost is *not* miracles? First of all, because at the time of Pentecost miracles were not a *new* thing. They were part of the ministries of Moses, Elijah, Elisha, and Daniel in Old Testament times. King Saul and others, being overwhelmed by the Spirit, joined with Samuel's band of prophets in the activity of prophesying, which in my judgment was clearly something miraculous, analogous to speaking in tongues (1 Sam 19:18-24). In Numbers 11:16-30 the seventy elders chosen to assist Moses in leading the people of Israel were given a similar ability: "Then the LORD came down in the cloud and spoke to him; and He took of the Spirit who was upon him [Moses] and placed Him upon the seventy elders. And when the

35

Spirit rested upon them, they prophesied. But they did not do it again" (v. 25). Even before Pentecost the apostles themselves were given power to work miracles (Matt 10:1,8).

Second, miracles did occur on and after Pentecost, but not *because* of Pentecost. God simply continued to give them as needed, which he had always done. They are not *special* to the Christian age. The apostles had miraculous powers before Pentecost, and they continued to work miracles after Pentecost, as needed.

> Miracles did occur on and after Pentecost, but not *because* of Pentecost. They are not special to the Christian age.

In fact, for a significant period of time after Pentecost, the apostles were the *only* ones in the church who were specifically said to be working miracles, even though the Holy Spirit was promised to all who accepted Christ and were baptized (Acts 2:38-39). Thousands were baptized (Acts 2:42; 4:4) and received the Spirit (Acts 5:32), but for a long time there is no mention of anyone working miracles *except* the apostles, who had this power before Pentecost. See Acts 2:43; 3:6; 4:33; 5:12-16. In due time there arose the need for others to receive miraculous gifts, but such were passed along through the selective, postbaptismal laying-on of the apostles' hands (Acts 6:5-8; 8:6,13,18). In any case, none of these miraculous powers was a new kind of thing.

Why were there miracles on the Day of Pentecost, then? We should remember that miracles are never the main event in any situation. Their purpose is always to point to and confirm a message from God; they function as evidence of the truth of the claims of God's messengers (see Mark 2:10; John 20:30-31; Acts 2:22; 2 Cor 12:12; Heb 2:3-4). This is why there were miracles (i.e., tongues) on Pentecost. They were given to confirm the truth and reality of *the* main event of Pentecost, i.e., the coming of the Holy Spirit as an abiding, indwelling presence for the new age.

We should carefully note this fact: the purpose of the Pentecostal tongues was *not* to enable the apostles to preach the gospel to the assembled audience. This was not necessary; all spoke Greek, which was a kind of universal language in that era.

Since all were Jews, it is also likely that they all could speak and understand Aramaic. Either way they seemed to be able to communicate with one another (Acts 2:5-13).

The bottom line is that the purpose of speaking in other languages on Pentecost was not to communicate a particular message, but to serve as evidence of the truth of the message Peter would preach in Acts 2:14-40 (a message in a common language understood by all). The impact of the tongues on the audience was *amazement* and *wonder:* they "were bewildered" (Acts 2:6); "they were amazed and astonished" (v. 7); "they all continued in amazement and great perplexity, saying to one another, 'What does this mean?'" (v. 12). The result of the tongues was not faith in Christ, because Peter had not yet preached the gospel. Their purpose and result was simply to *confirm the message* Peter was about to preach. They had a similar function in the meeting of Cornelius (see Acts 10:44-48).

> Miracles are never the main event. Their purpose and result is to confirm the message.

We can better understand the role of the tongues-speaking on Pentecost by comparing it with the "prophesying" in Numbers 11:16-30. When God instructed Moses to choose 70 elders to assist him in leading the Israelites, he specifically said, "I will take of the Spirit who is upon you, and will put Him upon them; and they shall bear the burden of the people with you" (v. 17). By putting his Spirit upon these 70 men, God would bestow upon them the gifts of wisdom and leadership. These were not miraculous powers.

On the appointed day the men gathered at the tent of meeting. "Then the LORD took of the Spirit who was upon him [Moses] and placed Him upon the seventy elders. And when the Spirit rested upon them, they prophesied. But they did not do it again" (v. 25). At the point in time when the Spirit was placed upon them to equip them for leadership, they were also given a one-time miraculous power to prophesy. Here we see a clear distinction between the actual giving of the Spirit (to equip for service, in this case), and the miraculous prophesying that served as a *sign* that the deed was done. In other words, the miraculous prophesying had the same evidential purpose as the tongues on Pentecost; namely, it was a one-time proof that God was keeping his promise concerning the bestowing of the Holy Spirit. This time it was to show that he was endowing these men with the gift of the Spirit for leadership purposes.

Note that verse 25 says that this miraculous prophesying happened only on this occasion: "they did not do it again." The King James Version says that their prophesying "did not cease," but this translation is based on a faulty Hebrew manuscript. More recent translations agree that the best manuscript reading is "they did not do it again;" even the New King James Version says, "Although they never did so again." This temporary nature of the miraculous accompaniment is likewise parallel to the tongues on Pentecost.

The bottom-line conclusion is this: *why should the miraculous manifestations on Pentecost (and later with Cornelius) be considered the essence of the new-age outpouring of the Holy Spirit? These kinds of things were nothing new!*

The Real Meaning of Pentecost

Throughout the Old Testament era, up to the Day of Pentecost itself, the Spirit was given to selected individuals to *equip* them with such skills and abilities as were necessary for service. The Spirit came *upon* them, but did not dwell *within* them. This was only an external presence and was not directly related to the individual's salvation. Even an unbeliever could be given this kind of spiritual gift (assuming that this was Saul's status in 1 Sam 19:20-24).

What God was promising to give to believers in the new age, however, was the *inward* presence of the Spirit: the indwelling, life-giving, sin-killing, soul-strengthening gift of the Spirit himself. As Ezekiel 36:27 prophesies, "I will put My Spirit within you and cause you to walk in My statutes." Jesus promised that true believers would have the Holy Spirit flowing from within them like rivers of living water (John 7:38-39).

> God's gift of the Spirit is his life-giving, sin-killing, soul-strengthening indwelling.

38

What, then, was given to God's people on Pentecost for the very first time? Not miracles, not even the forgiveness of sins, but the indwelling of the Holy Spirit! This was the day the Spirit was first poured out and made available to God's people in this way. This was the fulfillment of the prophecies made through Isaiah, Ezekiel, and Joel. This was the fulfillment of the promises made by John the Baptist and by Jesus himself. This is the true pentecostal power: spirit-given *moral* power to be good, to resist sin, and to witness with boldness (Acts 1:8).

Peter specifically identifies the outpouring of the Holy Spirit as the promise being fulfilled on that day: "Therefore having been exalted to the right hand of God, and having received from the Father the promise of the Holy Spirit, He has poured forth this which you both see and hear." When he said in Acts 2:39, "For the promise is for you and your children and for all who are far off," he was referring to the promised Spirit, as stated at the end of verse 38, "and you will receive the gift of the Holy Spirit."

Yes, there were miracles on Pentecost—the miraculous gift of tongues, the "prophesying" of which Joel spoke (Acts 2:16-18). But this was merely incidental and evidential in relation to the *real* gift of Pentecost—the Holy Spirit himself! The role of the miraculous tongues was to be the sign or evidence that this was indeed the beginning of something new—the initial outpouring of this new gift of the Spirit, which has been continuously present within the church since that day.

The initial giving of the Spirit was called "the baptism of the Holy Spirit," and on that occasion (as later with Cornelius) it was accompanied by miraculous tongues for evidential purposes. But the giving of the Holy Spirit to *every* individual believer at baptism is likewise called "the baptism of the Holy Spirit" (1 Cor 12:13). This term has no necessary connection with miraculous gifts.

This is how we should read the second chapter of Acts. The tongues event (vv. 1-13) was a sign that something big was about to happen. Peter's sermon (vv. 14-40) explained what this "something big" actually was: Jesus was keeping his promise to send the

Holy Spirit (v. 23; see 1:4-5), a promise which was offered to all who would repent and be baptized in Jesus' name (vv. 38-39).

Conclusion

We must put Pentecost, miracles, and the indwelling Spirit in the proper perspective. Those who see Pentecost's main significance as the miraculous tongues are simply missing the point. To see these powers as the essence of Pentecost does not do justice to the pregnancy of the promise. From the standpoint of the early church it would have been a great let-down, a disappointment something like opening a golden, bejeweled treasure chest and finding in it only a few jelly beans.

To put it another way, those today who still focus on the tongues aspect of Pentecost are like someone who receives a beautifully-wrapped birthday gift. After carefully removing the velvet ribbon and the expensive paper, the lovely box is opened to reveal the keys to a fancy new Mercedes automobile! But then this confused celebrant nonchalantly tosses aside these keys with a casual "That's nice." Then he turns back to the wrapping in which they came. "Wow! What wonderful ribbon!" he cries. "What beautiful paper! What a gorgeous box! I love it! I'm going to keep this ribbon and box and paper forever!"

We must be careful not to confuse the Pentecostal gift with the wrappings in which it came.

~4~
THE HOLY SPIRIT
AND THE SINNER

The Day of Pentecost marked a general historical transition regarding the way the Holy Spirit works. In the Old Testament era his main work was to equip selected individuals for roles of service to the body of God's people in general. In the New Testament era he continues to do this; but a new dimension has now been added to his work, one that relates specifically to salvation from sin.

In this chapter and the next two, this saving work of the Spirit will be explained. In this and the next chapter we are focusing on what the Holy Spirit does in the life of an individual sinner in order to bring that sinner into a state of salvation. In the following chapter we will examine how the Spirit works in the lives of Christians to enhance our spiritual growth.

How does the Spirit work upon the heart of the sinner?[1] This question must be divided into two parts. First, how does the Holy Spirit work to bring a sinner to faith and repentance? Second, how does the Spirit work upon the heart of the sinner *during* the moment of conversion itself, i.e., in the moment when the sinner makes the transition from the unsaved to the saved state? Here we are concentrating on the Spirit's preconversion work.

> The Holy Spirit exerts an influence upon the hearts and minds of sinners. How does he do this?

It is a fact that the Holy Spirit exerts an influence upon the hearts and minds of sinners, with a view toward bringing them to faith and repentance. How does he do this?

The Holy Spirit Works through the Word

Sinners are saved by grace, through faith (Eph 2:8). The faith that saves has two parts. It includes first of all what is often called *assent*, which is a judgment of the mind or intellect that a particular statement is true. The biblical terminology for this is "believing that" something is true (see John 8:24; 20:31; Rom 10:9; Heb 11:6). Saving faith also includes what is often called *trust*, which is a decision of the will to act upon the truth to which the mind assents. It is a personal surrender to the implications and consequences of this truth. Since the assent aspect of saving faith is primarily about the person and work of Jesus Christ, the trust element is a commitment or surrender to Jesus as Lord and Savior. The biblical terminology for such trust is "believing in" or "believing on" the person of Jesus Christ (see John 3:16; Acts 16:31; 1 Tim 1:16).

Sinners are also saved by repentance (Mark 1:15; Luke 13:3; Acts 2:38). The Greek word for repentance is *metanoia*, which means "a change of mind." Saving repentance is especially a change of mind about sin. As a change of mind, repentance obviously includes an intellectual act, namely, accepting the truth that we are sinners against God and under condemnation to eternal hell. Like faith, saving repentance also includes an act of the will. It is a change of mind in the sense of a change of our *attitude* toward sin. The heart and core of repentance is an inward hatred of sin and a sincere desire to be rid of it; thus it includes a commitment and determination to forsake sin.

> The heart and core of repentance is an inward hatred of sin and a sincere desire to be rid of it.

What is able to generate such faith and repentance in the hearts of sinners? The primary instrument and power by which this is accomplished is the Word of God, both in its form of law and especially in its form as gospel. As Paul testifies, "For I am not ashamed of the gospel, for it is the power of God for salvation to everyone who believes" (Rom 1:16). "Faith comes from hearing, and hearing by the word of Christ" (Rom 10:17). The Word is powerful enough to pierce the most callous heart: "For the word of God is living and active and sharper than any two-edged sword, and piercing as far as the division of soul and spirit, of both joints and marrow, and able to judge the thoughts and intentions of the heart" (Heb 4:12). The Word is like a seed which, when planted, can grow into faith (Luke 8:11-15; Jas 1:18,21). As Peter says, "For you have been born again not of seed which is perishable but imperishable, that is, through the living and enduring word of God" (1 Pet 1:23). The very purpose of the written Word is "so that you may believe that Jesus is the Christ, the Son of God, and that believing you may have life in His name" (John 20:31).

How does the Word of God generate faith and repentance? First, it informs our intellects of the truth concerning sin and salvation, the assent to which is the foundational element of both faith and repentance. By its very nature as written, verbal teaching, it accomplishes this purpose. But the power of the Word is more than the power of truth as such. There is also a moving and stirring force in the very facts of the gospel that are recorded in the Word. The message of how Christ died for our sins and arose from the dead, along with other biblical accounts, has the power to stir our emotions and prod our wills to make the decisions that are also necessary elements of faith and repentance.

Thus without the Word of God, there would be no faith and no repentance, and therefore no salvation.

But what does this have to do with the *Holy Spirit*? This question takes us back to the main subject of chapter 2 above, namely, the role of the Spirit in the origin of the Bible. Because of his works of revelation and inspiration, God the Holy Spirit is the ultimate author of everything in the Bible. Therefore, whatever is accomplished by the biblical message is ultimately accomplished by the Spirit himself. The Spirit influences the hearts of sinners by working on them indirectly through his own inspired Word.

> Whatever is accomplished by the biblical message is ultimately accomplished by the Spirit himself.

On the eve of his crucifixion, when Jesus was promising to send the Holy Spirit as a Helper or Advocate to his Apostles, he

43

said of the Spirit that "He, when He comes, will convict the world concerning sin and righteousness and judgment" (John 16:8). The word for "convict" is *elengcho*, which means "to expose, to bring to light, to convict or convince [of something]." Here the *parakletos* or "advocate for the defense" plays the role of prosecuting attorney against the world, exposing its sinfulness and convincing it of its need for a solution to God's righteous judgment.

How does the Spirit do this? It is no accident that this teaching about the convicting activity of the Spirit (John 16:8-11) is followed immediately by Jesus' promise that the coming Spirit of truth would guide the Apostles into all truth (John 16:12-15), that is, through his activity of revelation and inspiration. This seems to imply that these facts about the Spirit are linked together as effect and cause. That is, the Spirit will convict the world by means of the inspired teachings of the Apostles and Prophets. Through the Spirit-inspired Word, the light of truth is placed before the sinner, so that he is urged to believe and repent, and so that he knows he is condemned if he does not.

This connection between the work of the Spirit and the power of the Word is seen in Acts 7:51-52, where at the end of his sermon to the unrepentant Jewish leaders Stephen accuses them of "always resisting the Holy Spirit; you are doing just what your fathers did" when they persecuted and killed the prophets who preached to them. This strongly implies that when the Word of God is resisted, the Spirit himself (as the author of the Word) is also being resisted. On the other hand, when the Word succeeds in producing faith and repentance, it succeeds as an instrument of the Holy Spirit which he prepared for that very purpose (see John 20:31).

This is what we mean when we say that the Holy Spirit works (indirectly) through the Word of God to bring sinners to faith and repentance.

The Holy Spirit Works through Special Providence

Is there any sense in which the Holy Spirit may work *directly* upon a sinner's heart? The answer to this question is *yes*, the Spirit may work upon a sinner's heart through acts of *special divine providence*. Whatever may be involved in this, though, one must never think that it happens apart from the Word or instead of the Word. Rather, such providential activity is always *along with* the working of the Word as described above.

> **Providential activity always happens along with the working of the Word.**

What do we mean by "special divine providence"?[2] Our understanding of providence begins with the fact that the sovereign God has complete knowledge of and is in complete control of everything that happens, both in the natural world and in human history. The great majority of events are simply monitored and permitted by God via what is sometimes called his "general providence." However, if God so chooses, he may intervene in the flow of world events and cause things to happen that would not have happened without his intervention. Some of these things are miraculous, i.e., they are contrary to the laws of nature. Some are not contrary to the laws of nature but still take place only through God's special intervention. These latter events are sometimes called God's "special providence."

In acts of special providence God may manipulate natural processes: e.g., he may cause a drought or bring rain, or he may heal a sick person. Or God may work within a person's thought processes, e.g., by bringing forgotten ideas or facts to one's consciousness, in order to influence that person toward making a certain decision.

Though I am presenting this concept of special providence as part of the work of the Holy Spirit, I must qualify it thus: divine providence is not necessarily the exclusive work of any one person of the Trinity. Acts of special divine providence may indeed occur in the

> **Divine providence is not necessarily the exclusive work of any one person of the Trinity.**

45

life of a sinner to urge him toward faith and repentance, and these may indeed be the work of the Holy Spirit. But such providential intervention is not limited to God the Spirit; it is not one of his unique works.

With this qualification in mind, we may certainly affirm that the Holy Spirit does work upon the sinner's heart through providential means. How might this happen? For one thing, by his manipulation of events in nature and in the lives of other people, the Spirit may confront the sinner with circumstances that disturb him, or that cause him to think seriously about his life, or that "put the fear of God into him," as we sometimes say.

This may involve something drastic, such as natural disasters, personal sickness, accidents, or tragedy involving a loved one. I remember hearing a Christian man say, "Thank God for my heart attack." The attack came upon him when he was an unbeliever. He had to lie in bed quietly for six weeks while recovering. During that time he could not help but think about his close call with death, his wrong relationship with God, and his bleak prospects for eternity. He came under conviction and was converted. We do not know this for sure (since only inspired prophets can give sure interpretations of providence), but it is possible that God may have caused this heart attack for this very purpose.

Another example of how the Spirit may bring conviction through special providential intervention is an account told by a missionary who was active in China when this country was taken over by communists.[3] The missionary was arrested and subjected to severe questioning and mental torture. Throughout the procedure he would continually utter a quotation from the Psalms, "My times are in Thy hands." In what he describes as his "final ordeal," he was offered a knife and tempted to take his own life. He responded, "My times are in Thy hands." He reports, "The screaming voice of the interrogator demanded to know where the words came from and he threw a Bible before his victim. The sacred volume fell open at Psalm xxxi . . . . Here was a description of the present situation in detail" (see vv. 4,11,13-15,18,23-24). In the midst of the open page was the very quote the missionary had been saying all along: "My times are in thy hand" (v. 15). "This was too much for the still superstitious inquisitor who fled from the room." The missionary was then released and allowed to go home. The inquisitor did not come to saving faith and repentance, but he clearly was convicted of sin, righteousness, and judgment.

How do we explain the fact that the Bible, flung down on a table by the enemy, happened to open at that very place? The sovereign God has the power to manipulate muscles and wind currents; making sure the book opened to this text was an easy act of special providence.

Not all providential events will be this dramatic. For example, the Spirit could work upon a sinner's heart by causing him to hear a specific meaningful song as he scans stations on his car radio. Or the Spirit may providentially lead him to cross paths with an unexpected person who will be able to touch his heart.

In addition to confronting the sinner with convicting external circumstances, the Holy Spirit's special providences may involve working directly within the sinner's heart by keeping certain thoughts on his mind. We sometimes speculate that the devil tempts us by bringing evil ideas into our consciousness. If this can happen, then it is even more likely that the Holy Spirit may cause certain good memories to haunt our minds, pressing us to conviction. Examples may include the memory of a convicting song, or a convicting statement or look from an acquaintance, or the memory of a loving spouse's example and prayer (see 1 Cor 7:16; 1 Pet 3:1-2), or the memory of an appropriate sermon or Bible text.

What can the Spirit accomplish by such special providences (along with the Word)? Certainly such activity may make the sinner more responsive to the Word, thus "opening his heart" to the power of the gospel (see Acts 16:14). Such events may help the sinner to better understand the Word, in the manner described in the second part of chapter 2 above. Or they may simply soften a sinner's resisting will in ways that we do not understand.

47

This does not mean, however, that the Spirit's providential urgings will infallibly and irresistibly produce faith and repentance. The decision is still up to the sinner, whose will is free to say yes or no. Sometimes providential warnings are ignored or go unheeded, as is made clear in Amos 4:6-12. Here the prophet declares that God had been sending drought and pests and plagues of various kinds against Israel, "'Yet you have not returned to Me,' declares the LORD" (vv. 6,8,9,10,11). Clearly the purpose of this providential activity was to lead the Israelites to repentance, but they closed their minds to it and did not go where it was meant to lead them.

Nevertheless the Spirit does work upon sinners' hearts, both via the Word and via special providence. There are two very practical implications from this. First, if we do not believe the point about special providence, why do we pray for the lost? What do we expect to happen? What do we expect the Holy Spirit to do? We must expect him to do *something*, or we would not pray such prayers. And if we *do* believe that God can answer such prayers, why do we not pray more often and more fervently for the lost?

Second, in view of how the Spirit works in bringing sinners to faith and repentance, we should be more conscious of his role in the evangelistic process. Many Christians are filled with doubts about their ability to win sinners to Christ; many do not even attempt it for fear of failure. But we should remember that the success of our evangelistic efforts is not really in our hands; it does not depend upon how clever and how professional we are as "soul-winners." We must simply sow the seed of the Word (Matt 13:3-9); we must simply "go into all the world and preach the gospel to all creation" (Mark 16:15), remembering that there is a greater power at work in our preaching and witnessing than our own puny reason and oratory.

> There is a greater power at work in our preaching and witnessing than our own abilities.

The other side of this coin is that we should not get puffed up when we do lead someone to the Lord, as if this is accomplished by our great knowledge and expertise. As a young minister I often went calling with revival preachers. I remember one instance when the evangelist and I sat at a kitchen table with a Christian man and his unbelieving wife. As a result of this sharing of the gospel with this lady, we rejoiced to see her come to faith and repentance, and I baptized her later that evening. As we left this couple's house after this evangelistic visit, the revival preacher turned to me and asked, "What do you think I said that caused her to make her decision?" My first thought was, maybe it was not "something you said"; maybe it was simply the power of the gospel. I don't think I voiced that sentiment aloud, and maybe I was reading too much into his question. But it did impress upon me the need to rely upon the power of the Spirit in evangelizing.

Two Cautions

Before closing this chapter we must identify two extreme and incorrect views of how the Holy Spirit works upon the hearts of sinners. Each of these views must be avoided.

One is the view that every sinner is totally depraved and therefore must be supernaturally *caused* to believe by an irresistible act of the Holy Spirit. This view originated with Augustine in the early fifth century A.D., and persists today especially in that form of Christendom known as Calvinism.

This view says that as a result of Adam's sin every child is conceived and born in a state of total depravity. This means that no one has free will in the sense of an ability to respond to the gospel. Therefore, if it is left up to human decisions, no one will be saved. The only way anyone can be saved is for God to supernaturally cause sinners to believe and repent.

Now, if God wanted to, he could cause every individual to believe and repent and therefore to be saved. But for reasons of his own, God decides to save only some sinners, leaving the rest to go to hell. Those whom he decides to save (the "elect") are given the gift of faith by a special inner working of the Spirit which they are not even seeking. This is called "irresistible grace."

Once the elect person has been saved, God will unconditionally keep him saved forever ("once saved, always saved").

Those who accept this idea believe that the Holy Spirit always works in conjunction with the Word, but the power that brings the sinner to faith is neither the Word nor the sinner's own will. It is the unilateral power of the Holy Spirit alone.

In reference to the work of the Holy Spirit in the heart of the sinner, we must without hesitation or qualification reject this Calvinistic view. Total depravity is a false doctrine.[4] Sinners *are* depraved, but not totally so; they still have the free will to accept the gospel, especially as influenced by the power of the Spirit as he works through the Word and through special providence. His working, though, is always universal and resistible, contrary to Calvinism's view that his work is selective and irresistible.

> An unsaved sinner still has a free will with which to accept or reject God's salvation.

The second extreme that must be avoided is the idea that the Holy Spirit works on the sinner's heart through the Word of God *alone*, and not also through special providence or any other means. This view is often found in the Restoration Movement. Here the aversion to Calvinism is so strong that many have gone to this opposite extreme in order to avoid it. For our present purposes it is sufficient to say that the issue between Calvinism and the Bible is *not* whether the Holy Spirit works directly or indirectly upon the sinner's heart. Rather, it is whether his working is selective and irresistible (as in Calvinism) or universal and resistible. We affirm the latter.

NOTES

1. I am using the term "sinner" in the sense of an *unsaved* person, someone who is still under the power of sin and in a state of guilt and condemnation.

2. On the subject of providence, see my book, *What the Bible Says about God the Ruler* (Joplin, MO: College Press, 1984; now published by Wipf and Stock, Eugene, OR). Chapters 3–5 deal with general and special providence.

3. See "One Man with God," *The Presbyterian Journal* (Dec. 28, 1966), 9-10.

4. See my book, *The Faith Once for All* (Joplin, MO: College Press, 2002), 197-200.

≈5≈
THE HOLY SPIRIT AND CONVERSION

Acommon way of referring to a person's becoming a Christian is to say that he was *converted*. The Bible sometimes speaks of this event as a *turning*, i.e., a turning away from sin and a turning toward God (Acts 14:15; 11:21; 26:18). We might think of such conversion as including the entire process by which an unbeliever becomes a Christian. In this chapter, however, I am using the word "conversion" to refer only to one precise moment in that process, namely, the exact moment when the unsaved person becomes saved.

In the preceding chapter our subject was the work of the Holy Spirit prior to conversion. We asked the question, specifically what does the Spirit do to help bring about faith and repentance in the sinner's heart? Here our question is different. We are now asking, what does the Spirit do in the very moment of conversion itself? It is very important to distinguish these two questions.

> **What does the Spirit do in the very moment of conversion?**

What we shall see here is that in conversion the Holy Spirit performs a supernatural act upon the sinner's heart, an act that is part of the total package of saving grace which the sinner receives in that moment.

The Nature of Conversion

Exactly what happens to the sinner when he makes that all-important transition from being lost to being saved? Several specific things take place simultaneously. First, the sinner is justified or forgiven of his sins (1 Cor 6:11; Col 2:13). This is a change in his status before the law of God. The result is that he is relieved of his legal obligation to pay the debt of eternal punishment owed to God because of his sins. Second, at the same time that the sinner becomes justified, he is also regenerated or born again (Titus 3:5; Col 2:13). This is a change in the very nature of his heart. This means that his spirit or inner man is no longer in a state of spiritual death but is now alive toward God. Third, the sinner also at this time undergoes what is called initial sanctification. This is a one-time event in which the person is "set apart" in the sense that he ceases to be a member of Satan's kingdom and becomes a member of God's kingdom (1 Cor 6:11; Col 1:13). It is similar to adoption, or the moment when the sinner becomes a member of the family of God (Gal 4:5-7; Eph 1:5).

Our focus here is on the second of these saving acts, *regeneration*. Regeneration is not a change in our legal status before God, which is justification. It is not a positional change; that is adoption or initial sanctification. Nor is it a moral change, i.e., a voluntary change of mind and heart that the sinner himself accomplishes through an act of his own will as motivated by the gospel. Such a moral change is basically what faith and repentance are. This change is distinct from regeneration but is a necessary prerequisite for it.

> Regeneration is a metaphysical change, a change that takes place in the very essence of the soul.

What kind of change is regeneration, then? It is a *metaphysical* change, a change that takes place in the very essence of the soul. This does not mean that the soul's essence is somehow transformed into a different kind of stuff. It means simply that the damage sin inflicts upon the soul begins to be repaired; it means that the sin-sickness that infects the soul begins to be healed. By analogy it is the kind of change that takes place in an infected, feverous body when antibiotics are applied.

To follow this analogy, in the act of regeneration God assumes the role of the Great Physician (rather than the role of Judge as in the work of justification). Ezekiel 36:26 prophetically describes this work in terms of a heart-transplant operation: "Moreover, I will give you a new heart and put a new spirit within you; and I will remove the heart of stone from your flesh and give you a heart of flesh." Here

> In the act of regeneration God assumes the role of the Great Physician.

the "heart of stone" is the soul hardened and calcified by sin. It is removed and replaced by "a heart of flesh," that is, one that is soft and yielding to the will of God.

This event of regeneration is described in the Bible in several other ways. In Romans 6:1-14 Paul speaks of it as a death and resurrection: a death to sin and a resurrection to new life. As a result of this event the sinner is "alive from the dead" (v. 13) and able to "walk in newness of life" (v. 4). See Col 2:12-13; 3:1.

Other images are used to convey the same general concept. In Colossians 2:11 it is called an act of spiritual circumcision, "a circumcision made without hands" (see the prophecy in Deut 30:6). In John 3:3-8 Jesus speaks of regeneration as a new birth, being "born again" (see 1 Pet 1:3,23). Another strong image depicting the new-life nature of regeneration is that of *new creation* (2 Cor 5:17). Those saved by God's grace are "God's workmanship, created in Christ Jesus" (Eph 2:10).

All of these analogies—new life, new birth, new creation—not only picture regeneration as a time of new beginnings, but also show that it is an act that can be accomplished only by God.

The Holy Spirit Causes Regeneration

This leads us to our main point, namely, that the saving event known as regeneration is specifically the work of the Holy Spirit. The New Testament pictures the Spirit as the source and giver of life. "It is the Spirit who gives life; the flesh profits nothing" (John 6:63; see 2 Cor 3:6). He is called "the Spirit of life" (Rom 8:2). He is the "living water" (John 4:10; 7:38), i.e., the water that gives life. When he enters the sinner's heart, he brings resurrection from the dead. The sinner is born again into new life through the Spirit's power (John 3:5). The regeneration and renewing that occur in the heart are from the Spirit (Titus 3:5). The gift of the Holy Spirit promised in Acts 2:38 is the same as the "times of refreshing" in Acts 3:19.

Jesus promised the inward presence of this living water, but John explained that it would not begin until after Jesus' ascension and enthronement (John 7:37-39). This regenerating act of the Holy Spirit is thus a major aspect of the package of new benefits bestowed upon the church on the Day of Pentecost as the result of the outpouring of the Holy Spirit. There is no evidence that Old Testament saints received this aspect of salvation. It is a blessing enjoyed exclusively by Christians in the New Covenant age; it is a main reason why the Spirit has been given to us.

I am affirming here that in regeneration the Holy Spirit causes a literal change in the sinner's heart at the moment of conversion by acting directly upon the heart. This is contrary to a fairly common view in the Restoration Movement, going back to Alexander Campbell himself. Campbell said that regeneration is a *moral* change accomplished only *indirectly* by the Holy Spirit through the influence of the Word of God. For Campbell, regeneration is actually the sinner's own personal decision to believe and repent, a decision motivated by the Word but nonetheless accomplished by the sinner himself. Thus, in effect, the sinner regenerates himself, raises himself from the dead, recreates himself. This view has been voiced by many others.

This idea must be strongly rejected. In the Bible regeneration is a work of God, not a work of man. We are spiritually reborn into God's family "not of blood nor of the will of the flesh nor of the will of man, but of God" (John 1:13). Our death with Christ and resurrection with him are "the working of God" (Col 2:12).

| Regeneration is a work of God, not a work of man. |

In our new-creation natures "we are His workmanship" (Eph 2:10). The biblical images chosen to represent this mighty act—resurrection, new creation, new birth—in themselves point to divine activity; they are hardly feats we are capable of accomplishing by our own puny strength.

There is a real sense in which our death to sin and resurrection to new life are brought about by the saving power of Christ's death and resurrection, when that power is directly applied to our sinful hearts (Rom 6:1-14; Eph 2:5-6; Col 2:12-13). In this connection the Holy Spirit is the agent of regeneration because his work is to *apply* the saving benefits of Christ's death and resurrection to the sinner. He is the person of the Trinity who brings the power of Christ's death and resurrection to bear upon us.

The Holy Spirit Causes Regeneration in Baptism

In this chapter I have been referring to conversion as the precise moment when a sinner passes from his unsaved state to his saved state, but thus far I have not identified exactly when this moment occurs. I now affirm that conversion from the unsaved to the saved state takes place during the act of baptism. Thus the Holy Spirit works the work of regeneration in Christian baptism. The sinner is immersed into the baptismal water unregenerated, and emerges from it regenerated.

The Bible clearly teaches that regeneration occurs in baptism. Paul's teaching in Romans 6:1-4 could not be more clear. In this passage the Apostle is showing why it is a moral contradiction for a Christian to "continue in sin" (v. 1). This makes no sense at all, he says, in view of the fact that we have literally "died to sin" (v. 2). Surely you are not ignorant of what happened to you in your baptism, he suggests. "Or do you not know that all of us who have been baptized into Christ Jesus have been baptized into His death?" (v. 3). Baptism into Christ Jesus is a baptism into his death, i.e., into a union with the saving power of that death. This saving power includes not only the power to take away the penalty for our sins, but also the power to deal a death-blow to our indwelling sin itself. Baptism is thus the moment of our own death to sin: "Therefore we have been buried with Him through baptism into death" (v. 4). We cannot simply ignore the fact that

55

he says this death takes place "through baptism." Paul then says that this union with Christ in his death results immediately in union with him in his resurrection, enabling us to "walk in newness of life" (v. 4).

In a similar way Paul pinpoints the time of our regeneration as the moment of baptism in another text, Colossians 2:12: "Having been buried with Him in baptism, in which you were also raised up with Him through faith in the working of God." The references to "buried" and "raised up" reflect the proper form of baptism, immersion; but this is not their main point. "Buried with Christ" and "raised up with Him" again are referring to the saving event of regeneration, when "He made you alive together with Him" (v. 13). When does this saving event occur? Again it could not be more plain: "in baptism"!

This helps us to understand the meaning of Titus 3:5, "He saved us, not on the basis of deeds which we have done in righteousness, but according to His mercy, by the washing of regeneration and renewing by the Holy Spirit." Here Paul specifically refers to "regeneration and renewing" (synonymous terms) as a salvation event: "He saved us"; and he connects it with our "washing," i.e., the time of our baptism (see Acts 22:16). To understand this washing as a reference to baptism makes perfect sense in light of Romans 6:1-4 and Colossians 2:12.

We conclude that regeneration occurs during baptism, but not that it is the result of any inherent power in the water or in the act itself. It happens only through the power of God as he works upon the sinner's heart in that moment according to his promise.

What does this have to do with the work of the Holy Spirit? Alongside the above New Testament teaching that regeneration occurs in baptism, we also find the teaching that the Holy Spirit is given to us in baptism. In Titus 3:5 the "regeneration and renewing" that occur in baptism are specifically attributed to the Holy Spirit. God saves us, says Paul, by the *washing*. How is this so? Because it is a washing of *regeneration and renewing*. But how can the baptismal washing *be* a "washing of regeneration and renewing"? Because this regeneration and renewing are a work of *the Holy Spirit*! In verse 6 Paul identifies the Holy Spirit as the one whom God "poured out upon us richly through Jesus Christ our Savior." This reminds us of the Pentecostal outpouring, but it actu-

> We can properly think of our baptism as our own personal Pentecost.

ally refers to our personal baptism. Thus we can properly think of our baptism as our own personal Pentecost!

Another clear connection between baptism and the gift of the Holy Spirit is Peter's Pentecost sermon itself. When those convicted by his sermon cried out, "Brethren, what shall we do?" Peter replied, "Repent, and each of you be baptized in the name of Jesus Christ for the forgiveness of your sins; and you will receive the gift of the Holy Spirit. For the promise is for you and for your children and for all who are far off" (Acts 2:37-39). The promised Spirit is *for you* who are seeking salvation, he says. How may this salvation, including forgiveness of sins and the gift of the Holy Spirit, be received? Through repentance and baptism. Those who repent and are baptized will receive the gift of the Holy Spirit—not a gift *from* the Spirit, but the Spirit himself as an indwelling, healing presence. Peter was surely thinking of this instruction when later he declared that God has given the Holy Spirit "to those who obey Him" (Acts 5:32).

When we consider all of this data together—(1) that the Holy Spirit is the cause of regeneration, (2) that regeneration occurs in baptism, and (3) that the Holy Spirit is given in baptism—we must conclude that the Holy Spirit causes regeneration in the very act of baptism itself.

Those who object to such a conclusion will point to the many biblical references that say we are saved "through faith" (e.g., Eph 2:8). It is certainly true that faith is the *means* by which we receive salvation in baptism, but this does not contradict the fact that baptism is the *time* when this happens. Colossians 2:12 clearly affirms both: we are buried and raised up with Christ "through faith," but "in baptism." We should

> Faith is the *means* by which we receive salvation in baptism, but this does not contradict the fact that baptism is the *time* when this happens.

remember that "through faith" does not mean "as soon as you have faith."

Another objection usually follows, though. This is the claim that the passages that relate baptism to regeneration are not referring to *water* baptism but to *Spirit* baptism, or baptism in the Holy Spirit, which is believed to occur "as soon as we have faith." This objection in effect says that the Christian actually experiences two baptisms: one in the Spirit at the moment of faith (which is the saving event), and one in water at a later time. But this is in clear contradiction to Ephesians 4:5, which clearly says that there is but "one baptism" in the church's experience.

This raises the question, what is meant by the phrase, "baptism in (or by) the Holy Spirit"? This expression is used seven times in the New Testament. Four are the parallel Gospel accounts of John the Baptist's announcement of the Messiah, "I baptized you with water; but He will baptize you with the Holy Spirit" (Mark 1:8; see Matt 3:11; Luke 3:16; John 1:33). Two references in Acts (1:5; 11:16) are referring back to the original statement of John. The other reference is 1 Corinthians 12:13, "For by one Spirit we were all baptized into one body, whether Jews or Greeks, whether slaves or free, and we were all made to drink of one Spirit." First Corinthians 6:11 should also be considered, though it uses "washed" instead of "baptized." In all these references the terminology is the same. The verb "baptize" is modified by the prepositional phrase "in the Holy Spirit" or "in one Spirit." The Greek preposition is *en*, which can mean "in" ("with") or "by." The difference is not significant.

What is meant by this expression, "baptized in the Holy Spirit"? Many Reformation-oriented church groups take it as referring to the work of the Spirit when he bestows the new birth at the same moment when a sinner believes and repents. It is thus separated from water baptism. In Wesleyan-oriented church groups (especially holiness and Pentecostal) and also charismatic groups, "baptism in the Spirit" is taken as referring to a "second work of grace," which is an event that occurs after the initial reception of salvation and usually after water baptism. For some of these it is the time when the Spirit gives complete sanctification; for others it is the time when the Spirit gives the "Pentecostal blessing" of speaking in tongues or other miracles. Many in the Restoration Movement have taken "baptism in the Spirit" as referring only to the two events of Pentecost (Acts 2) and Cornelius's conversion (Acts 10). They say this mainly because they see "baptism in the Spirit" as inseparably connected with miraculous spiritual gifts, which they believe ceased after the first century.

I agree with none of the above views. As I see it, "Holy Spirit baptism" is something every Christian has experienced: "By one Spirit we were all baptized into one body." Its purpose is not to bestow miraculous powers, but to bestow the saving work of regeneration or the new birth. The miraculous manifestations at Pentecost and at Cornelius's conversion were unique excep-

> Spirit baptism and water baptism are the same event, the "one baptism" of Ephesians 4:5.

tions given for evidential purposes, and were not meant to be part of the essence of normal Spirit baptism.

In my judgment Spirit baptism and water baptism are the same event; the one baptism (Eph 4:5) has an outside and an inside (see Heb 10:22). At the same time that our bodies are baptized in water, our spirits are baptized in the Spirit.

The Result of Regeneration

Regeneration is a change in the sinner's nature, but it is not a complete change or a complete healing of the soul's sin-sickness. It is rather the reversal of the general direction of one's life. It is the beginning of a process of further change, the beginning of a lifelong healing process of sanctification. It is similar to an event often depicted in old Western movies where a principal in the story is wounded and develops an infection and a fever. With no antibiotics the local doctor can only monitor the sick man's condition until either the latter dies or "the fever breaks," as they would say. The time when "the fever broke" was the turning point, the beginning of the wounded man's recovery. Likewise, regeneration is the time when the Holy Spirit causes the sin-fever to break, and when his life-giving power sets the sinner on the road to spiritual wholeness.

The result of regeneration, then, is that the saved person can now say, "I *can* obey God's will; I *am able* to obey the law's commands"—which the unregenerated person was unable to do (Rom 8:7-8). We died and rose with Christ, "so that we would no longer be slaves to sin" (Rom 6:6). The spiritual heart transplant of which Ezekiel speaks (36:26-27) enables one to walk in God's statutes and observe his ordinances. "For we are His workmanship, created in Christ Jesus for good works" (Eph 2:10). That is, the ability to do good works is the very purpose and result of regeneration.

Thus "how shall we who died to sin still live in it?" (Rom 6:2). This would be like a man, after his fever has broken or his heart transplant has been successful, being content to lie in bed for the rest of his life. It would be like someone who has a new Mercedes in his garage continuing to ride a broken-down bicycle everywhere he goes. "May it never be!" says Paul (Rom 6:2). We have been *changed*—changed by the Holy Spirit, to continue to walk by the Spirit (Gal 5:16).

⁓ 6 ⁓
THE HOLY SPIRIT AND SANCTIFICATION

Ever since the Day of Pentecost the Holy Spirit has been working in the lives of God's people in a wonderful and exciting way. We have already discussed how he worked upon us before we were Christians, and how he worked within us in our conversion. The question now remains, how does the Holy Spirit work within the lives of individuals *after* we become Christians? What is the Spirit doing for us *now*?

> What is the Spirit doing for us now that we are Christians?

The key word is *power*. The Holy Spirit is giving us two different kinds of power. First, he is giving us *ministering* power in the form of spiritual gifts. These are skills or abilities that enable us to serve others within the body of Christ. This will be the subject of the next chapter. Second, the Holy Spirit is giving us *moral* power, enabling us to obey God's commands and live a godly life. He gives us *power for holy living*. That is the subject of this chapter.

The Indwelling of the Spirit

We commonly speak of the "indwelling" of the Holy Spirit. In the previous chapter we saw that the Spirit is active in the conversion experience of baptism. In fact, Acts 2:38 says that when a repentant sinner is baptized, he receives the Holy Spirit as a gift. We take this to mean that in the moment of baptism the third person of the Trinity, God the Holy Spirit himself, enters into our lives in a special way and remains there, using each individual Christian as a dwelling place.

61

The Reality of the Spirit's Indwelling

We accept the reality of the indwelling of the Holy Spirit because the Bible teaches it, using this very terminology. We will remember that the inwardness of the Spirit's presence was part of the pre-Pentecostal promise. It was prophesied in Ezekiel 36:27, "I will put My Spirit within you." Jesus said the Spirit would be like "rivers of living water" flowing up from the believer's innermost being (John 7:38).

In his writings the Apostle Paul uses the language of indwelling when describing how the Spirit is related to us. In a familiar passage (1 Cor 6:19) he says, "Or do you not know that your body is a temple of the Holy Spirit who is in you, whom you have from God, and that you are not your own?" Even though Paul uses plural pronouns here, it is clear from the preceding context that he is talking about the personal physical body of each individual Christian. The Greek word for "temple" is *naos*, which means a temple, shrine, or sanctuary associated with the divine presence. The Spirit is literally "in you," says Paul—the Spirit "whom you have from God," the one whom you received as a gift from God in your baptism. When you received him, he began to use your body as his dwelling place.

Paul uses similar language in Romans 8:9-11. "You are not in the flesh but in the Spirit," he says, "if indeed the Spirit of God dwells in you" (v. 9). The verb for "dwells" is *oikeo*, which is related to the noun *oikos*, meaning "house." To say that the Spirit of God "dwells in you" thus means that he treats your body as his house, his residence. He is not just paying you a visit; he has moved in to stay! Your body is where he lives! Paul continues in verse 11, "But if the Spirit of Him who raised Jesus from the dead dwells in you, He who raised Christ Jesus from the dead will also give life to your mortal bodies through His Spirit who dwells in you." Here he says twice more, in unambiguous language, that the Spirit "dwells in you." He says the same thing in

> The Holy Spirit makes each baptized believer his dwelling place in body and soul.

2 Timothy 1:14, where he speaks of "the Holy Spirit who dwells in us."

We must not conclude from these texts that the Spirit's presence within us is limited to our *bodies*. Two other texts declare that the Spirit is also within our *hearts*, which is a common biblical term for our soul or inner spiritual being. In 2 Corinthians 1:22 Paul says that God "sealed us and gave us the Spirit in our hearts as a pledge." He also says, "God has sent forth the Spirit of His Son into our hearts" (Gal 4:6).

These passages affirm the reality of the Spirit's indwelling, but they do not explain *how* he dwells in us. We know that it must be something more than simple divine omnipresence, by which divine being is present to all space equally. The Spirit's indwelling, however, is selective; he dwells only within Christians. Also, we must not identify the Spirit's indwelling with the fact that his inspired Word abides within us (Col 3:16; 1 John 2:24). Both kinds of presence are true, but they are two different things. We should also note that the divine Holy Spirit does not live within us in the same sense that a demonic spirit might invade and occupy someone's body. The latter spirit is a finite, created being and exists on an entirely different metaphysical level than the divine Spirit.

Though we cannot understand the *manner* of the Spirit's presence within us, we are convinced of its reality. What gives us this assurance? One serious caution is that our confidence in his indwelling must not be based on some kind of personal experience, such as a glowing feeling or an episode of tongue-speaking. Such experiences are *not* a guarantee of conversion and of the Spirit's presence (see Matt 7:21-23). Our assurance must be based, rather, on the simple promises of God's Word, which we accept by faith. We believe the Spirit is within us because this is what God promised to do in our baptism (Acts 2:38-39; see 5:32). We need no more assurance than this.

The Purpose of the Spirit's Indwelling

The Holy Spirit dwells within us—but *why?* Why did God initiate this great gift on Pentecost, and why does he continue to give the Spirit to those who are baptized into Christ? What is the purpose for the Spirit's continuing presence within us? This can be answered in a single word: *sanctification*. We will now explain this concept.

> **What is the purpose for the Spirit's continuing presence within us? Sanctification.**

The term "sanctification" is part of the word family having to do with holiness. The root idea in this word family is *separation*. The Old Testament word for "holy" (*qadosh*) most likely comes from a word that means "to cut, to divide, to separate." Thus a holy person or thing is one that is separated or set apart from others.

In the New Testament the main adjective for "holy" is *hagios.* Variations are the verb *hagiazo*, "to make holy, to set apart or consecrate, to sanctify"; and the noun *hagiasmos*, "holiness, sanctification, consecration." Thus sanctification is basically the same concept as holiness. We should also note that the adjective *hagios* is often used as a noun, i.e., "holy one." When used thus of Christians, it is usually translated "saint."

For Christians there are two main aspects of sanctification. The first, mentioned in the previous chapter, is *initial* sanctification. This refers to the one-time event in which the unsaved person joins the ranks of the saved, the moment in which he is set apart from "this present evil age" (Gal 1:4) and united with the body of Christ. This is the meaning of "you were sanctified" in 1 Corinthians 6:11, where the Greek verb is aorist tense, signifying a completed past action. This initial sanctification occurs at the same time that "you were washed," i.e., baptized.

This is the sense in which a Christian is a "saint," a "holy one," a "separated one." Saints are not an elite group of especially righteous Christians; every member of the body of Christ is a saint, a set-apart one, sanctified in this initial sense (Acts 9:13,32; Rom 1:7; 15:25-26; 1 Cor 1:2; Phil 1:1).

The second main aspect of sanctification is the one we are concerned with here. It may be called *progressive* sanctification because it is the ongoing process in which the Christian becomes more and more separated from sin itself. This aspect of sanctification is not a change in status or relationships, but a continuing transformation of our inward character and mental attitudes, as well as our outward behavior and conduct.

> The Holy Spirit accomplishes both initial and progressive sanctification in the indwelt believer.

This is how we "grow in the grace and knowledge of our Lord and Savior Jesus Christ" (2 Pet 3:18) and "work out [our] own salvation with fear and trembling" (Phil 2:12). In this aspect of sanctification we become more and more like God in righteousness and holiness of truth (Eph 4:22-24). Our pattern and goal are God's own ethical holiness, as we are commanded to imitate his perfect moral character: "But like the Holy One who called you, be holy yourselves also in all your behavior; because it is written, 'You shall be holy, for I am holy'" (1 Pet 1:15-16). As Jesus says it, "Therefore you are to be perfect, as your heavenly Father is perfect" (Matt 5:48). Our goal is to "share His holiness" (Heb 12:10), or to "become partakers of the divine nature" (2 Pet 1:4) in this moral sense. We are to purify ourselves, even as he is pure (1 John 3:3). See Luke 1:75; Rom 6:19,22; 2 Cor 6:14–7:1; 1 Thess 3:13; 4:7.

The fact that most of the passages just cited are exhortations to Christians (who have already been initially sanctified or set apart) shows that this aspect of sanctification is indeed a process and is appropriately called "progressive." This is also seen in Paul's prayer for God to complete the process in 1 Thessalonians 5:23, "Now may the God of peace sanctify you entirely."

How the Holy Spirit Sanctifies Us

After conversion, then, the Christian's primary task is to develop holy character and holy conduct. This is where the Holy Spirit enters the picture. His primary work in our Christian lives is to help us to become more and more holy. As Don DeWelt once said, "When the Holy Spirit took up residence within us, He did so with the thought of aiding us in developing holy character." What he made possible for us by regenerating us, he now makes actual for us through sanctification.

Sanctifying Knowledge

How does the Spirit do this? We said earlier that the Spirit does two main kinds of work: he gives us knowledge and he gives us power. Both are involved in the sanctification process. We already saw in chapter 2 that the Spirit gives us knowledge by giving us the Bible. The knowledge we derive from Scripture is absolutely necessary for sanctification. To become holy, we must know what holiness is. To vanquish sin and remove it from our lives, we must know what God has declared to be sinful. The only sure way we can know these things is through the Spirit-inspired Word. "All Scripture is God-breathed and is useful for teaching, rebuking, correcting and training in righteousness, so that the man of God may be thoroughly equipped for every good work" (2 Tim 3:16-17, NIV). See chapter 2 for more on how the Spirit can help us to understand Scripture.

Sanctifying Power

Our main focus here is that the Spirit sanctifies us by giving us *power* for holy living. In developing a holy character, our biggest problem is not lack of knowledge but lack of power. Our *knowledge* of what is right usually exceeds our *doing* of what is right. As Paul said of himself in Romans 7:19, "For the good that I want, I do not do, but I practice the very evil that I do not want." Our minds are informed, but our wills are weak. We need spiritual or moral *power*.

> The Spirit sanctifies us by giving us power for holy living.

This is where the indwelling Spirit comes to our aid. He dwells within us not to give us more knowledge, nor to provide our intellect with new information. Rather, he is present in us to

66

empower and strengthen our wills so that we may overcome temptation and sin, obey God's commands, and do good works.

Described in negative terms, sanctification means that we must be "putting to death the deeds of the body" (Rom 8:13). These are the sinful deeds that result from the law of sin that continues to reside in our flesh, in our as-yet-unredeemed bodies (Rom 6:6; 7:18,23-25). These sins must be put to death, killed, destroyed, overcome, driven from our lives. This eradication of sin is the Christian's personal responsibility: "If . . . *you* are putting to death the deeds of the body." It is not automatic and inevitable; we must personally will and do it. Paul's main point, though, is that we will not accomplish this alone but only "by the Spirit." The indwelling Spirit is the key to our victory over sin. On our conscious level we are aggressively putting sin to death, but below the level of our consciousness the Spirit's energizing power is making it possible.

> The indwelling Spirit is the key to our victory over sin.

Described in positive terms, sanctification means that we must obey God's commands and work out our salvation in fear and trembling (Phil 2:12). This means that the overwhelming responsibility to be holy as God is holy predictably fills us with awe and trepidation. What a daunting task! But this is why we must not stop reading this text at verse 12 but must also read verse 13, "For it is God who is at work in you, both to will and to work for His good pleasure." God has indeed commanded us to pursue sanctification (Heb 12:14), but he has not left us to do this from our own resources alone. He himself, in the person of the Holy Spirit, is at work in us, to help us both to *want* to do what is right ("to will") and to help us actually to *do* it ("to work").

> The Holy Spirit helps us both to want to do what is right and to actually do it.

The sanctifying power of the indwelling Spirit is the substance of Paul's prayer for us in Ephesians 3:16, where he prays that God "would grant you, according to the riches of His glory, to be strengthened with power through His Spirit in the inner man." This is a clear reference to the moral power provided to us by the indwelling Spirit. We ourselves should join with the Apostle Paul in praying that the strength of this power will help us to overcome specific sins and to develop specific virtues. When strengthened with power from the Spirit, we produce the fruit of holiness (Gal 5:22-23).

Leading and Filling

The New Testament describes the sanctifying power of the Spirit in different ways. For one thing, it says the Spirit *leads* us. "For all who are being led by the Spirit of God, these are sons of God" (Rom 8:14; see Gal 5:18). We "walk by the Spirit" (Gal 5:16) or walk "according to the Spirit" (Rom 8:4). Galatians 5:25 exhorts, "If we live by the Spirit, let us also walk by the Spirit." The NIV translates this last part, "Keep in step with the Spirit." In Romans 4:12 this same word is translated "follow in the steps of" (NASB) and "walk in the footsteps of" (NIV).

What does it mean to be "led by the Spirit"? Many have assumed that it means that the indwelling Spirit somehow gives us *knowledge* about what decisions God wants us to make when we are faced with difficult choices, that he enlightens our minds in some subjective and mystical way, that he "guides" us by inwardly showing us God's will in specific circumstances.

I believe this is a seriously false understanding of the Spirit's leading. With reference to *knowledge*, the Holy Spirit has already given us adequate guidance in the words of the Bible. The leading that comes from his indwelling is not a subjective enlightenment of the mind but an inward empowerment of the will. He gives us the inner strength to be "putting to death the deeds of the body," as Romans 8:13 explains verse 14. He does this through an inward prodding of the conscience, encouraging our wills to do what we already know is right based on the teaching of Scripture. The Spirit thus leads us by taking our hand and gently pulling us along the path of righteousness.

The New Testament also speaks of being *filled* with the Spirit. Paul exhorts us in Ephesians 5:18, "Do not get drunk on wine, which leads to debauchery. Instead, be filled with the Spirit" (NIV). Many have misunderstood this passage as referring to the alleged "second work of grace," described as our postconversion "baptism in the Spirit." This view says that at conversion only some of the Spirit's blessings are given; in the later event of filling, we receive the rest of his blessings. For many this includes an all-at-once completion of the process of sanctification, so that the Spirit-filled person now lives above sin. For others it includes miraculous powers, especially the ability to speak in tongues.

In my judgment this is *not* the meaning of "filled with the Spirit." What Paul is referring to here is the ongoing sanctifying work of the Spirit, with special emphasis on our responsibility to make sure this happens. In sanctification, our own wills must be employed. The Spirit's sanctifying power is within us, but we must take the initiative to use it and apply it. Beginning with conversion, we already have present and available to us everything the Spirit provides for holy living. Our responsibility is to take advantage of his help, to allow him to lead us, and to follow in his steps as he runs interference for us against our spiritual enemies.

In Ephesians 5:18 the verb is imperative; we are *commanded* to be filled. We do not sit back and wait for it to happen; it is our responsibility. It requires our submission and cooperation. The verb is also a *present* imperative, signifying continuing, ongoing action. Thus "to be filled with the Spirit" means to take full advantage of the already-present and available power of the Spirit who resides within us. In terms of our bodies or our lives as the house in which the Spirit dwells, it means that we must open up *all* the rooms in this house to the Spirit's presence. We must give him access to and control of all parts of our lives. Until we do so, we are not *filled* with the Spirit.

> "To be filled with the Spirit" means to take full advantage of the already-present and available power of the Spirit who resides within us.

In this light we can understand Paul's exhortation, "Do not grieve the Holy Spirit of God" (Eph 4:30). We grieve the Spirit when we ignore his sanctifying power and continue in our sin. See 1 Thess 5:19.

Claiming the Power of the Spirit

We know that God commands us to be holy as he is holy (1 Pet 1:15-16), to work out our own salvation (Phil 2:12), and to pursue sanctification (Heb 12:14). We also know that he has given us his Spirit for the very purpose of making this possible. Our question now is this: on a practical level, how may we personally appropriate the Spirit's power and allow him to work within us? The following is an eightfold path leading to this end.

(1) The first step to sanctification is *information*. As we have said, to be holy we must learn from Scripture what constitutes sin and what constitutes holiness. This is the sense in which God's Word is a lamp to our feet and a light to our path (Ps 119:105). Using the teaching of God's Word we can know what the ideal Christian life is, how we measure up in its light, and where we must change.

(2) The second step is *awareness*. We must be aware from Scripture *that* the Holy Spirit is within us, and *why* he is in us. Building this awareness has been the subject of this chapter.

(3) The third step is *desire*. We must have a sincere desire to be rid of sin and to be holy. We cannot approach sanctification simply as an obligation; we must really want to achieve it.

(4) The fourth step is *prayer*. This is a very important part of the process. It is not so much a separate step, but is rather something that must be done in conjunction with every other step. For example, we must pray that God would increase our desire to be holy (step 3), realizing that the Spirit himself can work within our hearts to increase this desire. Also, sanctifying prayer must be applied to specific sins and specific virtues. We might, for example, seek God's special work in our lives with the request, "I pray that the Spirit will give me the power to overcome my impatience," or anger, or lust. Such prayer must be strenuous, fervent, and persistent.

(5) The fifth step is *surrender* to the Spirit's power, with the acknowledgment that our own willpower is not sufficient. This is

70

a confession of personal weakness and helplessness, and a total reliance upon the Spirit.

(6) The sixth step to sanctification is *trust*. We must believe that the Spirit really will help us, that he will provide the needed power to do what is right. We truly are "sanctified by faith" (Acts 26:18).

(7) The seventh step is *action*. We are not robots; we have free will. We must not expect the Holy Spirit to take possession of our bodies as a demon might or even as the Spirit himself has done in causing individuals to speak in tongues. In pursuing holiness we must make the decisions, and we must make an effort to resist temptation and to do right. We must act, trusting the Spirit's power to make it possible. We must obey Philippians 2:12 in the light of Philippians 2:13.

(8) The final step is *thanksgiving*. We must thank God for the wonderful gift of spiritual power and give him the praise and credit for every victory over sin and every advance in holiness.

~7~
THE HOLY SPIRIT AND SPIRITUAL GIFTS

Now that we are Christians, what is the Holy Spirit doing for us? Two things: he is sanctifying us, as we saw in chapter 6, and he is equipping us with special gifts by which we may serve others, which is the subject of this chapter. In reference to both regeneration (ch. 5) and sanctification, the Spirit himself is the gift bestowed upon us so that he may perform these saving works within us. In his equipping ministry, the Holy Spirit is the one who bestows upon us gifts of service. Here we will refer to the latter as "spiritual gifts."

There are other biblical words for "gift," but the one generally used in this connection is *charisma* (plural, *charismata*), from which we get our English word "charismatic." In the New Testament this word is used for both miraculous and nonmiraculous gifts. Paul says that "we have gifts [*charismata*] that differ according to the grace given to us" (Rom 12:6). Peter says, "As each one has received a special gift [*charisma*], employ it in serving one another" (1 Pet 4:10).

In this chapter we will explain the concept, the purpose, and the types of spiritual gifts.

The Concept of Spiritual Gifts

What does it mean to say, "I have received a spiritual gift"? What constitutes "spiritual giftedness"? A common approach says that all Christians should examine themselves, discern their God-given strengths and abilities, and dedicate these as gifts from the

What does it mean to say, "I have received a spiritual gift"?

Spirit to service in the Kingdom. This personal-inventory approach is certainly relevant, but it is not the whole picture; indeed, it is not even the main point of spiritual gifts.

The mistake most commonly made is to equate natural gifts with spiritual gifts. Most people have certain innate or natural talents. Some are related to music, such as an aptitude for singing or playing the piano. Other people are artistically or athletically inclined. Some have intellectual gifts; others are natural-born leaders or have a gift of oratory. Some are especially good with numbers; others seem to have an innate empathy that makes them good at working with people, especially people in need.

It is important to recognize that most people have such natural endowments, whether they are Christians or not. Many use their abilities in the service of mankind (e.g., Albert Schweitzer, Thomas Edison); others use them selfishly for their own benefit or even for evil purposes (e.g., Adolf Hitler, Fidel Castro). The fact that such inclinations or tendencies or talents are present does not make them spiritual gifts. They are usually the result of good genes and/or good early environment. At best we may call them

Inborn abilities are not spiritual gifts. The primary aspect of a spiritual gift is not a talent but a task.

providential gifts. This means that God at least in his general providence has permitted such talents to be present, or that he in his special providence has tweaked one's genes or environmental circumstances to cause a special talent to develop. But the mere possession of inborn abilities, no matter how distinct and strong, does not constitute spiritual giftedness.

I am convinced that the primary aspect of a spiritual gift is not a *talent* but a *task*. One may indeed have a special talent for leading, for teaching, for encouraging, or for serving; and the presence of such a talent may be a factor in the spiritual gift bestowed by the Spirit upon any Christian. But the main point of receiving a spiritual gift is to be given a specific *task* to perform within the body of Christ, whether one has an outstanding, innate ability for that task or not.

The key to identifying one's spiritual gift is to be *called* by the Spirit into a particular task or office or role of service. In Bible times when God worked through such supernatural means as revelation and inspiration, such calling was given directly to some individuals, e.g., Moses (Exod 3:1-9) and Saul of Tarsus (Acts 9:3-9). Sometimes the calling was made by God's people, guided by general instructions from God (e.g., Num 11:16; Acts 6:3).

Such calls are issued to people who may or may not have an outstanding ability for the specified task. When miraculous gifts are involved, such as tongues or healing, an innate ability will by nature be absent. People do not have *natural* abilities to do *supernatural* things. Regarding nonmiraculous gifts, most often we can expect the Spirit to call someone who already has some relevant providential ability. When this happens, the role of the Spirit is to enhance,

> **People do not have natural abilities to do supernatural things.**

sharpen, and focus that talent for the task to which the person is being called.

The following are some examples of this concept of spiritual gifts, beginning with two important Old Testament accounts. We should remember that the equipping work of the Holy Spirit was present in Old Testament times; his new work beginning with Pentecost was the inward saving activity of regeneration and sanctification.

The first example has to do with the building of the tabernacle or tent of meeting shortly after the Israelites received the Mosaic Law from God on Mount Sinai. A main part of God's instruction from Sinai was a detailed description of how to build the tabernacle. Constructing this house of God was no small undertaking, and required the assistance of people who knew how to work with wood, metal, cloth, and precious stones. Where were such skilled artisans to be found? Here is God's plan (Exod 31:1-6):

> Now the LORD spoke to Moses, saying, "See, I have called by name Bezalel, the son of Uri, the son of Hur, of the tribe of Judah. I have filled him with the Spirit of God in wisdom, in understanding, in knowledge, and in all kinds of craftsmanship, to make artistic designs for work in gold, in silver, and in bronze, and in the cutting

75

of stones for settings, and in the carving of wood, that he may work in all kinds of craftsmanship. And behold, I Myself have appointed with him Oholiab, the son of Ahisamach, of the tribe of Dan; and in the hearts of all who are skillful I have put skill, that they may make all that I have commanded you."

See also Exodus 35:30–36:2.

From this we may learn several things about how the Spirit of God bestows spiritual gifts. First, through Moses God called two men by name to oversee this task of building the tabernacle: Bezalel and Oholiab. Because these men were in charge of the entire project, it appears that the Spirit gave them at least *some* new skills, making them experts in all aspects of the work. He even gave them the ability to teach these crafts to others (Exod 35:34). This indicates that if a person is available for God's calling, the Spirit can indeed give him or her the ability needed for the task even if it was not already providentially present.

Second, the workers called for individual tasks do seem to have had some already-present skills; but when they answered God's call, God enhanced and consecrated their skills and made them even better at their tasks. God declares, "In the hearts of all who are skillful [lit., "wise"] I have put skill [lit., "wisdom"], that they may make all that I have commanded you" (Exod 31:6; see 36:1).

Third, these craftsmen pooled their specific gifts in order to accomplish a common purpose of building the tabernacle or worship center. Each worker used his gift to meet this overall need of the group.

Finally, the main point is that these people were *called* to perform *tasks*. The talents, whether innate, learned, or bestowed, were secondary to the task.

How does this relate to spiritual gifts today? I believe this episode constitutes an Old Testament type or prophetic analogy of the meaning of spiritual gifts in the New Covenant era. In many areas, what was true of Old Testament Israel on a *physical* level has an intended counterpart in the New Testament Church on a *spiritual* level. The Old Covenant tabernacle (later, temple) pointed ahead to the Church of Jesus Christ, which is itself God's New Covenant temple (1 Cor 3:16-17). Just as the spiritual gifts given to the men in Exodus 31:1-6 were physical skills for building a physical building, so in New Testament times the spiritual gifts are of a more "spiritual" nature, since we are building up a spiritual building to the Lord (1 Pet 2:5). The concept and the purpose of the gifts are the same, however.

Another Old Testament example is the incident in Numbers 11:16-30, where 70 elders were called to assist Moses in leading the people. Again, the key idea is that they are being called to perform a *task*. In this case God instructs Moses to select the 70 men who would be given this task. He also gives Moses general instructions concerning who should be chosen for this responsibility. Those called must be men, men already known and recognized as leaders among the people (v. 16). "When the Spirit rested upon them" (v. 25), they became approved by God and equipped for a special role as leaders through the enhancement of their leadership skills.

Two New Testament examples may be cited. One of the main spiritual gifts listed by Paul (Eph 4:11; 1 Cor 12:28) is the office of apostle. In the early church, the Spirit called specific individuals to perform the task or function of apostles. God himself, in the person of Jesus Christ, issued this call. We are not told anything about special abilities already possessed by such men as Peter, Andrew, James, and John; but we know that Jesus called them and assured them that God would use them for a special work (Matt 4:18-22; see Matt 9:8). Saul of Tarsus was a man of considerable ability and education, but he was not an apostle until he was specifically called by Jesus to that office (Rom 1:1; 1 Cor 1:1). Once called, he was given special miraculous gifts that were "signs of a true apostle" (2 Cor 12:12).

The other New Testament example is the appointing of the seven servants in Acts 6:1-6. In the early church the need arose for someone other than the apostles to look after the needs of the many widows within the church. The Apostles instructed the

77

church, "Therefore, brethren, select from among you seven men
of good reputation, full of the Spirit and of wisdom, whom we
may put in charge of this task" (v. 3). In this situation the church
itself selected and called the seven men who would perform this
service. There is no indication that these seven had special talents
for this task; but they had to be men, men of good reputation and
known to be "full of the Spirit and of wisdom."

We conclude that a spiritual gift is a *calling to perform a task*
within the church. Having an *ability* for the task is good, but this
is not the crucial issue. The Spirit may call someone *with* a talent,
and then enhance and focus that talent toward the task. Or the
Spirit may call someone *without* a talent, and then bestow the ability upon him if needed.

In any case, having an ability does not in itself constitute having a spiritual gift. The important point is the calling. In Bible
times God himself called individuals for service, such as Moses
and the Apostles. Sometimes even then, and usually today, the call
comes only indirectly from God by means of the church or its rep-
resentatives. As we will see in the next chapter, in New Testament
times almost all miraculous gifts and tasks came indirectly,
through the laying on of the hands of the Apostles (Acts 6:6;
8:17-18; 19:6). Sometimes the church participates in the calling
through its representative leaders, such as the elders (1 Tim 4:14;
Acts 13:4; 15:22). Sometimes the call comes from the church col-
lectively (Acts 6:3; 15:22).

From all of the biblical examples it is important to see that
being given a spiritual gift, i.e., being called to perform a task, is
not some subjective, mysterious reality that we must anxiously
struggle to discern. Even when God called someone directly, he
did not do so with some ambiguous, mystical feeling. Thus today,
when we think about our own spiritual gifts, the first thing we
must consider is this: to what task is the church (perhaps through
the elders) calling me?

When the church thus participates in the bestowing of spiritual gifts (by calling individuals to certain offices and tasks), this

must always be done in accordance with the instructions and qualifications laid down by God in his Word. And the church must remember that the possession of an ability as such is not equivalent to possessing a gift from the Holy Spirit. Ability alone is not equivalent to "giftedness," especially where God's Word specifies certain limitations and qualifications for those who may be called to certain tasks. See 1 Timothy 2:9–3:13.

> **Ability alone is not equivalent to "giftedness."**

The Purpose of Spiritual Gifts

What is the purpose of spiritual gifts? Whether in Old Testament or New Testament times, the purpose is the same, namely, to equip individual Christians to meet the *needs* of God's people as a whole. In the Christian era the Spirit's regenerating and sanctifying work meets my needs as an individual; his equipping work is for the building up of the whole church. The Spirit gives gifts according to the needs of the body.

> **The Spirit gives gifts according to the needs of the body.**

Indeed, in the New Testament the main metaphor used to establish this point is the nature of the human body. Each part of the body has a specific function, and each part performs its function for the good of the whole body. Paul explains in Romans 12:4-5, "For just as we have many members in one body and all the members do not have the same function, so we, who are many, are one body in Christ, and individually members one of another." He says, "But to each one is given the manifestation of the Spirit for the common good" (1 Cor 12:7).

The body illustration explains why all Christians do not have the same gifts; there is a need for diversity and multiplicity of functions. "If the whole body were an eye, where would the hearing be?" (1 Cor 12:17). Also, this analogy shows that while some gifts may be more vital than others, all are needed for the well-being of the body as a whole (1 Cor 12:23-26).

But mainly the body metaphor clearly illustrates the purpose of each of the many kinds of spiritual gifts, namely, to meet a specific need for the harmonious functioning of all parts of the body together. Just as the members of our bodies do not exist and function independent of the other members, and do not simply serve themselves, so also do individual Christians not exist by themselves and for themselves. They do not use their spiritual gifts for their own gratification, but for making the complete body of Christ function smoothly and harmoniously. To do this we must recognize our interdependence, i.e., that we need the gifts exercised by everyone else, and that others need our gifts (1 Cor 12:21).

Paul states this purpose in 1 Corinthians 14:12, "So also you, since you are zealous of spiritual gifts, seek to abound for the edification of the church." This is how we are good stewards of the gifts bestowed upon us: "As each one has received a special gift, employ it in serving one another as good stewards of the manifold grace of God" (1 Pet 4:10).

A key word in this discussion is the word *need*. The Spirit gives gifts that meet the *needs* of the body. These needs do not remain constant. The things needed in one era are not necessarily needed in later times. Gifts needed in the Old Testament era, for example, are not all needed in the New Covenant age, e.g., the physical skills needed to construct the tabernacle, as explained above, or political leaders such as judges (Judg 3:10; 6:34; 11:29; 14:6,19; 15:14) and kings (1 Sam 10:1-13; 16:13-14). Likewise, in the early decades of the church certain gifts were needed that are not needed for the bulk of Christian history, as explained in the next section. In whatever era, the Spirit's gifts meet the church's needs.

> Some needs of the early church do not exist today.

Types of Spiritual Gifts

In the New Testament there are four main lists of spiritual gifts that have been bestowed in the New Covenant era, gifts given to and experienced by the church. These lists are in Romans 12:3-8 (7 gifts), 1 Corinthians 12:8-10 (9 gifts), 1 Corinthians 12:28-30 (9 gifts), and Ephesians 4:11 (4 or 5 gifts). See also 1 Peter 4:10-

11. Some of these gifts are obviously repeated from list to list, e.g., prophets or prophecy is in all four main lists. Some seem to be different words for the same gift, e.g., leading (Rom 12:8) and administrations (1 Cor 12:28). We need not conclude that these lists are exhaustive. For example, nothing about music is mentioned, nor are modern skills such as computer expertise.

In analyzing the gifts that are listed, it is appropriate to divide them into two main categories, based on the principle of *need* discussed above. In light of this principle we conclude that some of the gifts were meant to be *temporary*, since their need was temporary. Some, however, are meant to be *permanent*, since their need is permanent.

Temporary Gifts

Why do we conclude that some gifts were temporary? The first clue is that the office of *apostle*, which is included twice (Eph 4:11; 1 Cor 12:28), is a listed gift but obviously cannot extend beyond the first century in view of the qualification for the office given in Acts 1:21-22. Another clue is that Paul specifically says certain gifts "will cease" while the church continues (1 Cor 13:8-13), a point that will be discussed later.

When we reflect upon these and other facts, we will see that in the earliest years of the church there were certain needs that are not present today. These temporary needs arose basically from the lack of an authoritative written New Covenant revelation comparable to the Old Testament. The earliest Christians did not yet have a written New Testament. This created specific needs which the Spirit filled through temporary gifts, one of which was the task of apostleship. Being an Apostle meant receiving and communicating inspired revelation and other authoritative teaching from God to the church. This temporarily filled the need later met by the completed New Testament.

In the church's earliest days, not even the Apostles could be present in every local congregation. Thus other spiritual gifts

> Paul says that certain gifts "will cease," while the church continues.

comparable to those possessed by Apostles were given temporarily to various members of local churches wherever they were located. These gifts fall into two main categories. First, there were gifts of supernaturally given knowledge, providing Christians with access to the mind and will of God even when Apostles were not around. Prophecy (on all four lists) is the main such gift. A prophet was one who received inspired messages from God; the gift of prophecy is in no way equivalent to ordinary preaching. Other gifts of supernatural knowledge, likewise temporary, are wisdom (1 Cor 12:8), inspired knowledge (1 Cor 12:8; 13:2,8), discerning of spirits (1 Cor 12:10), and tongues when interpreted (1 Cor 12:10,28,30).

The other category of temporary gifts involves miraculous powers, the point of which was to provide evidence for the truth of the newly revealed teaching of apostles and prophets. This, of course, is always the purpose of miracles (see 2 Cor 12:12; Heb 2:3-4). Such gifts include miracle-working faith (1 Cor 12:9; 13:2), miraculous healing (1 Cor 12:9,28,30), general miracles (1 Cor 12:10, 28-29), and uninterpreted tongues (1 Cor 14:22).

Permanent Gifts

The remainder of the listed gifts are permanent gifts since their need is not related to the presence or absence of the written New Testament. Included here are gifts of leading or ruling in the church, which refers specifically to the office of elder. I believe this is what is intended in the gift of leadership (Rom 12:8), the pastors (or pastor-teachers) of Ephesians 4:11, and the gift of administrations (1 Cor 12:28).

Another main kind of permanent gift is the calling to teach and preach the Word. Teaching is mentioned three times (Rom 12:7; Eph 4:11; 1 Cor 12:29). A teacher is one who is able to aid the understanding by explaining what has been revealed through apostles and prophets. The gift of exhorting (Rom 12:8) seems to be the ability to speak with power to move the heart, conscience, and will. "He gave some . . . as evangelists" (Eph 4:11); this is the ability and calling to preach the gospel to unbelievers.

Other permanent gifts involve assisting and serving the church in various ways. The gift of general service is named in Romans 12:7 and 1 Peter 4:11. This may be the same as the gift of "helps" in 1 Corinthians 12:28. Both probably refer to the office or task of the deacon. More specific is the gift of giving (sharing) in Romans 12:8, which is the inclination to use one's own money and goods in acts of private benevolence. Finally, there is the gift of showing mercy (Rom 12:8), or using one's time and ability to bring comfort to the lonely, the sick, and the grieving.

> Spiritual gifts are given in order for God's people to accomplish specific tasks which meet specific needs.

In discerning one's own spiritual gift, one should listen first of all to the call God gives, not in some subjective, elusive way but through the church. Where does your church need you to serve? What has your church leadership asked you to do? Accept the call, and trust the Spirit to bring your abilities into line with the task.

⚜ 8 ⚜

THE HOLY SPIRIT AND MIRACLES TODAY

Within the boundaries of Christendom today, most believe that the Holy Spirit is presently active in the church, and that he is now working in the lives of individual Christians. Most believe that the Spirit acts upon sinners to regenerate them, and that he acts within Christians to sanctify them. Most believe that the Spirit also gives spiritual gifts to the members of Christ's body. There is a general unity on these issues.

One issue where there is serious disagreement, however, is the question of whether the Holy Spirit gives *miraculous gifts* to Christians today. Many claim that he does, some going so far as to say that you are not a true Christian unless you have spoken in tongues. Others argue that the Holy Spirit is *not* giving miraculous gifts to Christians today, and that he has not done so since approximately the end of the first century, when the last Apostle (John) died.

This latter view is sometimes called *cessationism*, since it argues that miraculous gifts have *ceased*, in the language of 1 Corinthians 13:8. This is my personal conviction. I believe that the Holy Spirit does *not* give gifts of supernatural knowledge and miraculous power to Christians today. This and the next two chapters will make the case for this view.

> **Cessationism argues that miraculous gifts ceased when the last Apostle (John) died.**

What Is a Miracle?

Some Christians get upset at the suggestion that miracles have ceased, because they do not have a clear understanding of what a

85

miracle actually is. Some think that anything God does is a miracle, or that any phenomenon that causes wonder is a miracle. One writer has claimed that "a miracle is anything that causes us to stop and acknowledge God's intervention in our ordinary human lives."[1] Things that may thus be called miracles, she says, include a rosebud, a sunset, a phone call from a loved one, and finding a needed dress on a sales rack. The author concludes, "Miracles are around us every day. Our life and breath are miracles of God's creative thought. . . . Surely, the least we can do is acknowledge His provision and call it by name—a miracle."[2]

The well-intentioned sentiments voiced in this article in *The Lookout* are certainly expressions of sincere piety. However, when measured by biblical teaching they must be called not just superficial but confused, confusing, misleading, and false. The author takes no account whatever of the way the Bible uses the terms for miracles, and apparently is not aware of what is at stake in defining miracles so loosely.

Others may not be so naive as to call a rosebud a miracle, but they still get upset at the suggestion that miraculous gifts have ceased, because they think this somehow puts limits upon God and upon his power. Some even assume that the cessation of miraculous gifts would mean that God cannot heal the sick today.

The problem with this kind of thinking is the assumption that every act of God—every divine or supernatural act—must be called a *miracle*. Thus if there are no miracles, then God is not

> All works of God are supernatural acts, but not all works of God are miracles.

acting. This is simply not true to Scripture. What is true is this: all works of God are *supernatural* acts, but not all works of God are *miracles*. To say it another way, all miracles are supernatural events, but not all supernatural events are miracles. Miracles are a quite narrow and specific kind of divine activity.

To give an overview, there are basically four kinds of events. First, some events fall under the heading of "general providence."[3] These are things that happen the way they do because of the way God created the world in the first place. They are the result of two relatively independent forces that God chose to bring into existence and which he allows most of the time to operate on their own. These forces are the laws of nature and free-will beings. Events that happen as the result of unaided natural law and human free-will choices are *not* caused by God, except indirectly insofar as he is the one who created this system to begin with. Rosebuds, sunsets, phone calls, and department store sales are usually in this category, as far away from true miracles as possible.

The other three kinds of events are all different from the above because all three *are* the result of God's divine intervention into the world. They are all acts of God and are thus all supernatural. However, not all of these are miracles. The first such kind of supernatural event (and the second overall kind of event) is what we call acts of "special providence."[4] These are the occasions when God intervenes in the course of nature and the flow of history, yet in ways that are so subtle that no one will actually observe or recognize them as supernatural. They occur within the boundaries of natural law and do not violate natural law, but they are nonetheless events that would not have happened without God's special causation. An example is the healing of a sick person in answer to prayer (Jas 5:16). This is something that still happens today, but it is not a miracle because from our perspective the healing process conforms to natural laws.

The second kind of supernatural event (and third overall kind of event) is what I call "supernatural spiritual events." These are very special works of God that do not involve the physical world and thus are beyond the very sphere of natural laws. These are things God does on the level of spiritual reality. They may happen in conjunction with physical events (e.g., as the atonement occurs in the crucifixion), but they actually occur in the dimension of spiritual reality (divine and human).

One kind of supernatural spiritual event is the *saving* works of God. This category includes the main redemptive works associated with Jesus: his incarnation, atonement, and enthronement at God's right hand. It includes the outpouring of the Holy Spirit on

> **The supernatural "saving works" of God include the main redemptive works in the earthly and ongoing heavenly ministry of Jesus.**

Pentecost. It includes works of salvation applied to us as individuals: forgiveness, regeneration, the Spirit's continuing indwelling. Strictly speaking these are not miracles, because they are outside the realm of the physical and thus cannot be observed by our senses.

The other kind of supernatural spiritual event is God's *revelatory* activity, especially the Holy Spirit's work of revelation and inspiration within apostles and prophets. The main purpose of this supernatural activity is to give us revealed explanations concerning the reality and meaning of the saving works of God mentioned in the previous paragraph. In other words we could never know that Jesus of Nazareth is the incarnate Son of God, or that his death on the cross makes us right with God, unless these truths had been revealed to us by the Holy Spirit in Scripture. Such revelatory activity is definitely supernatural, but still not miraculous.

The third and final category of supernatural events (and the fourth overall) is *miracles.*[5] Like the last two categories, miracles are acts of God; but they are unlike the other two categories in crucial ways. Miracles are unlike supernatural spiritual events because they are visible acts occurring on the level of the physical. Also they are unlike acts of special providence because they are

> **Miracles must be visible as proof of God's truth.**

obviously contrary to natural law. For example, instead of a gradual healing brought about in answer to prayer, a miracle is an immediate healing of a lame or blind man. The reason why miracles must be visible events obviously contrary to natural law has to do with their purpose, which is to serve as *proof* or evidence of the truth of the claimed revelatory explanation of God's redemptive works. This will be explained further in the next section.

Thus we can see why we must be quite selective in what we call a "miracle." Many marvelous things happen in the world, and many of them are directly caused by God; but this does not mean they are miracles. We do not honor God when we call things miracles that are not.

Arguments against Miracles Today

Those who declare that the Holy Spirit is not giving miraculous gifts today do not do so arbitrarily or without reason. There are solid arguments against the reality of present-day miracles from God. These include the following.

The Purpose of Miracles

As stated under the last point, a main reason why miracles must be narrowly defined has to do with their purpose. Once we understand that purpose, we will see why God does not give miraculous powers today.

The New Testament uses three main words for miracles. One is the word for "power" (*dynamis*), which speaks of the *source* of the miracle, i.e., the supernatural power of God. This word is often translated "miracle." The second word is "wonder" (*teras*), which suggests the immediate *result* of a miracle, such as an unusual display of divine power that causes amazement and wonder. The third word for miracles is "sign" (*semeion*), which occurs often throughout the New Testament. This word sums up the ultimate *purpose* of any miracle. In Acts 2:22, 2 Corinthians 12:12, and Hebrews 3:4, all three of these words are used together.

Miracles are designed to function as signs. They serve the purpose of giving evidence (proof, confirmation) of the truth of the revelation which they accompany. They authenticate God's messengers and the truth of their messages. Jesus was proved to be who he claimed to be by his miracles, wonders, and signs (Acts 2:22). An example is his healing of the paralytic (Mark 2:1-12). He first forgave the man's sins (v. 5), an implicit claim to deity (v. 7). Then he declared before all, especially the skeptics, "But so that you may know that the Son of Man has authority on earth to forgive sins" (v. 10)—then he healed the man (vv. 11-12). "So that you may know" sums up the purpose of all miracles. John declares that some of Jesus' signs are recorded in his Gospel as evidence to

89

his readers of Jesus' divine identity and work: "Therefore many other signs Jesus also performed in the presence of the disciples, which are not written in this book; but these have been written that you may believe that Jesus is the Christ, the Son of God" (John 20:30-31). "So that you may believe" again sums up the purpose of miracles.

> "So that you may believe" sums up the purpose of miracles.

If miracles are signs, specifically what are they signs *of*? As stated, they are signs or evidence of the truth of what is claimed to be revelation from God. But this raises another question: under what circumstances does God give revelation? The answer is that he gives revelation in connection with his redemptive works: to predict them, to identify them, to explain them, to tell us how to respond to them. Such redemptive works include the Exodus events at the time of Moses, the cross and resurrection of Jesus, and the Pentecostal outpouring of the Spirit.

Analyzing the biblical data, we may conclude that these three things will always happen together: God's *redemptive works*, as explained by God's *revelation*, which is authenticated by *miracles*.[6] This pattern is reflected in Hebrews 2:3-4, "How will we escape if we neglect so great a salvation? After it was at the first spoken through the Lord, it was confirmed to us by those who heard, God also testifying with them, both by signs and wonders and by various miracles and by gifts of the Holy Spirit according to His own will."

How does this relate to the question of whether miracles are still occurring today? As long as God is performing new redemptive works, we can expect new revelation to be given in order to explain these new works. In this case we can then expect more miracles to happen to authenticate the new revelation. But once God's redemptive works have been accomplished, explained, and confirmed, we should not expect any further miracles. That is, we would expect miracles today only if new redemptive works are taking place, which is not happening. Thus the very purpose of miracles argues against their continuation beyond the first century.

> Once God's redemptive works have been accomplished, explained, and confirmed, we should not expect any further miracles.

The Laying On of Apostles' Hands

Another reason for denying the presence of miraculous gifts in the church today is the connection between one's receiving miraculous gifts and having an apostle's hands laid on him. This connection is established by the events recorded in the book of Acts.

In the earliest days of the church, though thousands were being baptized and thus were receiving the indwelling presence of the Spirit as promised (Acts 2:38-41; 4:4; 5:14,32), only the Apostles are said to be performing miracles (Acts 2:43; 3:6; 4:33; 5:12-16). Only after the Apostles laid their hands on the seven servants in Acts 6:1-6 do we have a record of anyone else—two of the seven—working miracles (Stephen, 6:8; Philip, 8:6-7,13).

The necessary connection between miraculous gifts and the laying on of Apostles' hands is clearly seen in Philip's ministry in Samaria in Acts 8. Though Philip was working miracles (after the Apostles laid hands on him in Acts 6), and though many were being converted, none of the converts was given miracle-working power until the Apostles Peter and John came down from Jerusalem "and prayed for them that they might receive the Holy Spirit" (v. 15). Though they had surely received the indwelling of the Spirit at their baptism, since that was God's general Pentecostal promise (Acts 2:38-39; 5:32), the Spirit had "not yet fallen upon any of them" (v. 16) in a miracle-giving way. Then the Apostles "began laying their hands on them, and they were receiving the Holy Spirit" (v. 17).

At this point a converted sorcerer named Simon "saw that the Spirit was bestowed through the laying on of the apostles' hands." This so impressed him that he tried to purchase this apostolic power with money, and thus experienced a fall from grace (vv. 18-24). The result of the laying on of the Apostles' hands could not have been the normal indwelling of the Spirit, since God had already promised this in baptism, and especially since the laying on of hands resulted immediately in something that Simon saw, something that was so spectacular that it led Simon to covet the power to bestow it, at the

91

risk of his salvation (vv. 18-19). It must have been a manifestation of miraculous abilities, especially speaking in tongues.

This is confirmed by the incident recorded in Acts 19:6, when the Apostle Paul laid his hands on the 12 Ephesian disciples, and they began to prophesy and speak in tongues.

These data lead us to conclude that there must have been a necessary connection between such miraculous manifestations and the laying on of Apostles' hands. The only two recorded exceptions to this are Pentecost and Cornelius, on which occasions the Spirit was poured out directly because of the need for a special kind of sign. Peter's words in Acts 11:15 suggest that what happened to Cornelius and his family (Acts 10:44-48) had not happened since Pentecost itself: no one else had prophesied or spoken in tongues without the laying on of Apostles' hands.

This leads to the conclusion that the bestowing of miraculous gifts must have ceased around A.D. 100, when John, the last Apostle, died.

A Biblical Declaration of Cessation

A final reason for saying that the Holy Spirit is not giving miraculous gifts today is that the Bible specifically declares that such gifts will cease. This was taught by Paul in 1 Corinthians 13:8-13, and will be explained in the next chapter.

Faulty Arguments for Miraculous Gifts Today

Those who believe miraculous gifts continue today (let's call them *continuationists*) have reasons for their view also, but I believe their arguments are faulty. Here I will summarize the problems with their reasoning. Most of these points have been covered in earlier chapters, so will not be dealt with in detail here.

First, continuationists believe that a main purpose of Pentecost was to make miraculous spiritual gifts available to all, especially the gift of tongues. I believe this is a faulty argument because it is based on a complete misunderstanding of Pentecost, as explained in chapter 3 above. The Pentecostal tongues were not normative and were not the main point of Pentecost. They were the accompanying signs of the true gift of Pentecost, the indwelling of the Holy Spirit for salvation purposes. Miraculous gifts could not have been the point of Pentecost, since Pentecost was for some great new gift of God and miracles were nothing new.

Second, continuationists argue that the purpose of the baptism in the Holy Spirit was to bestow miraculous gifts. Since Christians today are still experiencing the baptism in the Spirit, they must still be receiving such gifts. I believe, though, that this is a faulty interpretation of baptism in the Spirit, as explained in chapter 5. This is not an event separated from water baptism, and it is connected with salvation, not tongues.

Third, continuationists argue that miraculous gifts of different kinds are included in the various New Testament lists of spiritual gifts in general. They say there is no justification for thinking that just *some* of these gifts continue today. If some continue, they all must continue. On the contrary, I believe we have ample reason to distinguish temporary from permanent gifts, based on the principle of need, as explained in chapter 7. The next chapter will also be relevant here.

Finally, continuationists argue that miraculous gifts must be given today because they are actually happening within some Christian circles. People actually do speak in tongues, prophesy, and heal today. We cannot deny what is before our very eyes. My response to this will be given in chapter 10 below.

Problems with Modern Miracle Movements

In those groups where miraculous gifts are accepted today, especially within Pentecostal denominations and charismatic congregations, the very way these gifts are practiced raises questions about their validity when compared with biblical teaching about the Holy Spirit and about miraculous gifts. Several problematic characteristics of the modern practice of gifts will now be noted.

First, in these circles personal *experience* is elevated above the Word of God and is made the final norm for truth. The acceptance of miraculous gifts as authentic is based on their simple presence in people's experience. "I spoke in tongues; therefore the Spirit must be giving them today." But basing our convictions on our experiences rather than the Word of God is not only improper, but is also dangerous. See Matthew 7:21-23 and Luke 13:25-28.

> **Personal experience should not be elevated above the Word of God.**

Second, in charismatic and other such circles, the Holy Spirit is elevated above Jesus Christ, contrary to the Spirit's stated mission as one who will glorify Christ (John 16:14-15). Edward Fudge, in his booklet *Speaking in Tongues*, draws the following sober conclusion:

> Those claiming these gifts today nearly always exalt the Spirit above the Christ, preach their supposed experiences rather than the gospel of the Son of God, and (while in word denying it) actually become much more involved with the Holy Spirit than with the Son at the Father's right hand. This is a serious charge, but I do not make it lightly. I believe the evidence warrants such strong terms.[7]

Third, another serious problem is that miraculous manifestations occur today in a wide variety of church settings, within groups that teach contradictory doctrines. They are present in conjunction with all kinds of false doctrines and false religions. This creates a false sense of unity, and diminishes the importance of sound doctrine. Kurt Koch says it thus:

> In America, Jesuits, Lutherans, free church people, modern theologians, High Anglicans, and Mormons meet together in order to speak in tongues. They are convinced that this is true Ecumenicalism in action.
>
> This sounds fantastic. And yet I heard of a similar group in London. What a wonderful time we live in today! All schisms, all denominational barriers, age-long divisions have been overcome by the new gift of tongues. Does this really mean that what the Word

of God could not accomplish, has been brought about by a psychic epidemic?[8]

Hugh Pyle cites an example of "an Episcopalian priest in this city who is so liberal he neither believes in the virgin birth nor the resurrection. Yet he has recently received the baptism of the Spirit and exhibits a marvelous power in his ministry!"[9]

Fourth, at the same time that this superficial spirit of unity is being generated, many churches are being divided as a result of this movement.

Finally, modern tongue-speakers usually ignore the biblical rules for prophesying and speaking in tongues as given in 1 Corinthians 14. For one thing, the very point of women keeping silent in the church (14:34) is that they are not to use these gifts of prophecy and tongues in the public assembly. As Koch observes, "This is not heeded anywhere in the new tongues movement."[10] Koch also notes concerning 14:27, "Only two or three should speak in tongues on any one occasion. No notice is taken of this either in the new tongues movement. Ten, twenty, or even more people speak in tongues at the same prayer meeting."[11] An example of this is a recording in my possession of an Episcopalian service where the entire congregation is "singing" in tongues, all at the same time. Finally, contrary to 14:1 and 14:39, Koch says, "The gift of tongues is called the lowest gift by Paul, but today it is given first place by the tongues movement."[12]

The next two chapters will give further sound reasons for accepting the cessationist view.

NOTES

1. Josephine Manes, "Are Miracles for Today?" *The Lookout* (11/24/91), 13.
2. Ibid.
3. See Jack Cottrell, *What the Bible Says about God the Ruler* (Joplin, MO: College Press, 1983; now published by Wipf and Stock, Eugene, OR), chapter 3, "General Providence."
4. Ibid., chapters 4 and 5, on special providence.
5. Ibid., chapter 6, "Miracles."

6. See Robert L. Reymond, *What about Continuing Revelations and Miracles in the Presbyterian Church Today?* (Phillipsburg, NJ: Presbyterian and Reformed, 1977) 55-56.

7. Edward Fudge, *Speaking in Tongues* (Athens, AL: C.E.I. Publishing, 1971) 29.

8. Kurt Koch, *The Strife of Tongues* (Grand Rapids: Kregel, 1971) 25.

9. Hugh F. Pyle, *Truth about Tongues* (Denver: Accent Books, 1976) 23.

10. Koch, *Strife*, 39.

11. Ibid.

12. Ibid.

⚍9⚌
THE HOLY SPIRIT AND 1 CORINTHIANS 13:8-13

O ne of the strongest reasons for denying present-day miraculous gifts is the teaching of 1 Corinthians 13:8-13, especially verse 10: "But when the perfect comes, the partial will be done away." This verse specifically states that a time will come (in the future from the time Paul wrote these words) when certain miraculous gifts will cease.

The purpose of this chapter is to explain this passage, and to show that "the perfect" in verse 10 (*teleion* in Greek) is *the completed New Testament*. This means that when the New Testament writings were completed, miraculous gifts ceased.

> **When the New Testament writings were completed, miraculous gifts ceased.**

Strife over Tongues

The passage of Scripture we are discussing occurs in the midst of a larger section of the first Corinthian letter (chs. 12–14), a section in which Paul deals in detail with the whole subject of spiritual gifts. This entire letter shows that the church in Corinth had a number of internal problems. Paul is using his apostolic authority to address these problems and to exhort the church to straighten itself out. From what he writes in chapters 12–14, it is apparent that one of their problems was controversy over the use of spiritual gifts, especially the gift of tongues.

The Message of Chapters 12–14

In the very beginning of the letter Paul tells the Corinthians that he is aware of various divisions and quarrels within their congregation (1:10-11). One source of division was their attitude toward and practice of spiritual gifts. From chapter 12 we learn that these Christians had decided that there was a definite hierarchical order in the "varieties of gifts" (12:4), i.e., some gifts were regarded as more important and prestigious than others. Those who had such gifts enjoyed a higher status within the group, leading to division (12:25). For some reason they had concluded that the gift of tongues was the most important (see ch. 14).

The main point of chapter 13 is to put *all* of the spiritual gifts, especially the gift of tongues, into the proper perspective. All of the gifts are important and are not to be neglected (when properly used—14:20-40), but these gifts are not to be regarded as the most important aspect of the Christian life. Within the whole list of gifts prophecy seems most important, more important than tongues (14:1-19); but overall there are other aspects of the Christian life that are far more important than any such gifts. These are the things you should be concentrating on, says Paul; these are "a still more excellent way" (12:31).

In chapter 13 Paul explains that this "more excellent way" is *love*. Instead of fighting over these other gifts, such as prophecy, supernatural knowledge, and tongues, you *should* be focusing on loving one another. Love must be the matrix within which all other activities occur. Without love, nothing else matters (13:1-3).

> **Paul makes it clear that love is a more important spiritual gift than those relating to supernatural knowledge.**

To make his point Paul compares love (and later, faith and hope, v. 13) with the three representative gifts of prophecy, knowledge, and tongues. Why does he choose these three gifts? Because he wants to make a point, namely, that love is more important than even the most valuable of the spiritual gifts that he names in chapter 12, the gifts that are related to supernatural

98

knowledge. How does he show that even these gifts are relatively less important than love? By asserting that such gifts will come to an end, while love (and faith and hope) will continue to exist in the church's life.

Paul's challenge is this: Why are you getting so excited about things that are temporary? Why are you fighting among yourselves over things that are ready to pass away? Why are you dividing the church over things that will cease? "Pursue love!" (14:1).

The Structure of 1 Corinthians 13:8-13

The key section for our purposes is 13:8-13. It is very important to understand the outline or structure of this paragraph. It consists basically of *two contrasts.*

The first and main contrast is between things that are *temporary* (v. 8) and things that are *permanent* (v. 13). To get this point these two verses should be read together while setting verses 9-12 aside as a parenthesis, thus:

> Love never fails; but if there are gifts of prophecy, they will be done away; if there are tongues, they will cease; if there is knowledge, it will be done away. . . . But now faith, hope, love, abide these three; but the greatest of these is love.

Some things, Paul says, will cease—the very things you are fighting and dividing over: prophecy, knowledge, and tongues (v. 8). But the really crucial things will continue to exist—faith, hope, and love (v. 13a). The most important of all is love (v. 13b), since love *never* ends (v. 8a).

Paul could have written just this much and still have made his point. But he knew that he had to explain the temporary nature of tongues, etc., a bit further. He knew that in the minds of many Corin-

> The main contrast is between temporary and permanent gifts in the church.

thians the gift of tongues was the heart and soul of their faith. One can imagine their reaction to verse 8: "Oh, no, Paul! You can't mean that! Surely you are mistaken; surely tongues are not just temporary! Don't take away our tongues!"

99

In order to alleviate such concern, in verses 9-12, even before he completes his main contrast between verse 8 and verse 13, Paul inserts a *parenthesis* with a secondary contrast. Here the contrast is to show *why* gifts like tongues, prophecy, and knowledge are only temporary. The reason they are temporary, he says, is because they are only "partial" or piecemeal; something "perfect" or complete will come to take their place. This four-verse parenthesis should be read as a unit:

> For we know in part and we prophesy in part; but when the perfect comes, the partial will be done away. When I was a child, I used to speak like a child, think like a child, reason like a child; when I became a man, I did away with childish things. For now we see in a mirror dimly, but then face to face; now I know in part, but then I will know fully just as I also have been fully known.

Though the Corinthians no doubt did not want to hear this, Paul tells them that the very things they have made the centerpiece of their lives will be "done away" because they are only *partial.* As an analogy, their individual episodes of miraculous tongues and prophesying were like single pieces of a jigsaw puzzle. Something is coming, though, that will be like the entire puzzle with all its pieces put together; then you will see the entire picture. Will that not be much better?

What is this coming thing that will take the place of tongues and other such gifts? Paul calls it the *teleion* in verse 10, translated "the perfect." If we can just know what this *teleion* is, we can know *when* the tongues and other things will cease. This is true because Paul specifically says, "WHEN the *teleion* comes," the partial will cease.[1] The coming of the *teleion* will be the occasion for the end of these gifts.

The Identity of the *Teleion*

The case for the cessationist view of miraculous spiritual gifts rests to a large extent on our ability to identify the *teleion* to which

Paul refers in verse 10. We will now see how this can be done, based on the word itself and the context in which it appears.

Not "Perfect," but "Complete"

To determine what the *teleion* is, we must first consider the best English translation of the word in this context. The word is an adjective, and in this passage most Bible versions translate it "the perfect." (The original NIV has "perfection.") This is indeed one main meaning of the word, and it is properly so translated in other texts (e.g., Rom 12:2; Jas 1:17). The verb form of the word (*teleioo*) is often translated "make perfect" (e.g., Phil 3:12; Heb 7:28). Another main meaning of the adjective is "mature," and it is sometimes translated thus (e.g., 1 Cor 2:6; Eph 4:13). Still another main meaning is "complete," though the adjective and the verb are seldom translated thus in the New Testament. The NIV does translate the verb as "make complete" in several places (e.g., Jas 2:22; 1 John 2:5), and the TNIV translates *teleion* as "completeness" in 1 Corinthians 13:10.

Which of these meanings best fits the context of 1 Corinthians 13:10? Despite the fact that most Bible versions use "perfect," the obviously intended meaning in this verse is "complete." Why is this obvious? Because the *teleion* here is clearly contrasted with things that are *partial* (*ek merous*, "in part, of a part, partial")! Does it not make sense to contrast *partial* things with something that is *complete*? In my judgment this is a "no-brainer." Thus even though when reading most Bible versions we will encounter the word "perfect," in our minds we must think the word "complete."

> *Teleion* is clearly contrasted with things that are partial.

The Complete *Thing*

A second consideration is to recognize that *teleion* is a neuter adjective. Adjectives ordinarily modify nouns; but in this case no noun is given, thus it must itself be treated as a noun. In the Greek language adjectives and other parts of speech have different

> *Teleion* is a neuter adjective—it describes a "thing," not a person.

forms according to *gender*, i.e., they can be masculine, feminine, or neuter. If *teleion* here were in its masculine form (*teleios*), since it stands alone, we would translate it as "the complete one" or "the complete man," referring to a person. But in fact the adjective is neuter in gender, thus must be read as "the complete *thing*."

This is very important because some have seen the translation, "When the perfect comes," and have jumped to the conclusion that this must be a reference to the second coming of Christ. After all, Jesus is the only "perfect one," and he definitely is coming again! The implication regarding miraculous gifts, of course, would be that tongues, etc., will continue until the second coming of Jesus.

When we understand, though, that *teleion* is a *neuter* adjective, we will see that it refers not to a person at all, but to a thing. If it referred to a person such as Jesus, the gender would have been masculine. Thus the best translation is "When the complete *thing* comes." Paul is thus saying that the partial things will cease when the complete thing comes.

Not Connected with the Second Coming

Do we have any way of discerning what this complete thing is supposed to be? Yes. For one thing, we know the limitations as to the *time* when it will appear. On the one hand, since Paul uses future tense ("*will* cease . . . *will* be done away"), the *teleion* must still be in the future relative to the time Paul was writing this letter. This means that the complete thing cannot be *love*, since love was surely already present within the church to some degree. It is important to see this, since love has upon occasion been suggested as the identity of the *teleion*. But this cannot be.

On the other hand, we know from something Paul says here that the *teleion* must be something that will come *before* the end of the age, before the second coming of Jesus. This is extremely important, because the most common view as to the identity of the complete thing is that it must have something to do with the second coming and with heaven.[2]

How do we know that the complete thing must come *before* the end times and not in connection with the second coming? How do we know that it must come while the church is still existing in this age? Because of what Paul says in verse 13. Here he declares that the *teleion* will come and the partial gifts will cease while faith, hope, and love still abide or remain among God's people. If *hope* is still present, then the *teleion* must come before Christ's second coming, because once Christ comes, all that we are hoping for will become a *reality*, and hope itself will disappear. As Paul explains in Romans 8:24, we hope only for things we do not yet see, "for who hopes for what he already sees?" Some would apply this same reasoning to faith as well, since in one sense *sight* replaces faith (2 Cor 5:7) as well as hope.

In any case, verse 13 rules out any interpretation of the *teleion* that connects it with the second coming. Thus the partial gifts must cease sometime during the church age.

> The *teleion* will come and the partial gifts will cease while faith, hope, and love still abide or remain among God's people.

The Completed New Testament

A final consideration in our quest to identify the *teleion* is the fact that it is meant to *replace* some very specific kinds of gifts (v. 8). Since the complete thing replaces these partial things, it must be something similar in nature to the latter and must serve the same general purpose as the latter. What is the nature of the gifts named in verse 8? Prophecy, supernatural knowledge, and tongues (when interpreted) are all in the category of *revealed knowledge*. Thus the complete thing must also be in the category of revealed knowledge. Yet it is something *complete*, as contrasted with these partial forms.

Again this goes against identifying the complete thing as *love*, since love is not a revealed-knowledge kind of thing. Also, it rules out another view sometimes suggested, namely, that the *teleion*

103

should be translated "mature" and that the "mature thing" is really the *mature church*. Paul does seem to be contrasting childhood with maturity in verse 11, suggesting that the partial things are part of the church's childhood stage while the *teleion* is a mark of its maturity. But the specific identity of the *teleion* must be something other than the mature church itself, since the latter is not a kind of revealed knowledge.

The only thing that meets all the requirements pointed out in this section is *the completed New Testament*. The *teleion*, the complete thing, is the completed New Testament. When the completed New Testament has come, piecemeal prophecies, tongues, and knowledge will cease. This view is supported by the fact that elsewhere in the Bible God's will and word in the New Covenant era are described with this same adjective, *teleios*; see Romans 12:2; James 1:25; and

> **Elsewhere in the Bible God's will and word in the New Covenant era are described with this same adjective, *teleios*.**

Hebrews 5:14–6:1. Also, it is reasonable to think that Christians would be *expecting* a completed New Testament to guide them in this New Covenant age, in the same way that God's Old Covenant people had the Old Testament to guide them.

The New Testament was completed near the end of the first century, with the last writing of the Apostle John. All the New Testament books were then in circulation. Thus we must conclude that these partial gifts—tongues, prophecy, knowledge—*have ceased*.

The *Teleion* and 1 Corinthians 13:12

For many people a major problem in accepting the view that the *teleion* is the completed New Testament is what Paul says in 13:12: "For now we see in a mirror dimly, but then face to face; now I know in part, but then I will know fully just as I also have been fully known." At first glance this seems to be a contrast between our present condition and our future heavenly existence. This is what leads many to conclude that the *teleion* must be the result of the second coming.

In my judgment, however, this is a serious misunderstanding of verse 12. The time reference for the contrast between "now" and "then" is the time Paul was writing this letter. Thus the contrast is still between the church's years of piecemeal revelations ("now") and the time when the full New Testament will be available ("then").

> The contrast is still between the church's years of piecemeal revelations ("now") and the time when the full New Testament will be available ("then").

"In a Mirror Dimly" versus "Face to Face"

In the first part of the verse Paul contrasts two kinds of revelation, the less clear and the more clear. The less clear revelation is compared with trying to see one's face in a poor-quality mirror; the more clear revelation is compared with seeing one's face in a very good mirror. "For now we see in a mirror dimly, but then face to face."

The key to understanding this statement is Numbers 12:8. The similarity of the imagery and language of 1 Corinthians 13:12a and the Greek version of Numbers 12:8 is so strong that it is nearly certain that Paul has the latter in mind as he writes the former. In Numbers God is explaining to Aaron and Miriam why Moses as a prophet is in a class by himself compared with other prophets. God says he speaks with other prophets in visions and dreams, but with Moses "I speak mouth to mouth, even openly, and not in dark sayings." The phrase "mouth to mouth" here corresponds to "face to face" in 1 Corinthians 13:12a, and "not in dark sayings" corresponds to "dimly." In the latter phrasing the same Greek word is used in Numbers and in Corinthians, namely, *ainigma* ("riddle"). "In dark sayings" (Num 12:8) is literally "in riddles," and so is "dimly" in 1 Corinthians 13:12a.

For Moses and Paul the point is the same, i.e., a contrast between less clear and more clear revelation. Paul's image is definitely that of "seeing in a mirror." (The King James translation, "We see through a glass, darkly," is incorrect.) But he is *not* contrasting (1) seeing *only* as in a mirror, and (2) seeing in person, contrary to the NIV. The contrast is between (1) seeing in a cloudy, cracked mirror ("dimly"), and (2) seeing in a *clear* mirror where one's face can be clearly seen.[3]

Thus in 1 Corinthians 13:12 "dimly" versus "face to face" represents enigmatic, incomplete revelation versus clear, complete revelation. The former is the piecemeal, temporary prophecies and tongues; the latter is the completed New Testament. This is supported by 2 Corinthians 3:7-18 and James 1:23-25, where New Testament revelation is compared with looking in a mirror.

Some may still be hung up on the idea of seeing "face to face," thinking this must be a reference to seeing *Jesus* "face to face." Actually Paul does not say we shall see *him* face to face. There is no object for the verb "see," since no specific object is intended. The point is not what or whom we will see, but *how* we will see. It refers to the comparative clarity of the revelation in the completed New Testament.[4]

> The point is not what or whom we will see, but how we will see.

An expanded paraphrase of 13:12a is as follows: "For now, in these early days of the church, while we depend on occasional revelations through prophecy or interpreted tongues, it is like trying to see yourself in a scratched and cloudy mirror. But then, when the completed New Testament has come, it will be like seeing a sharp, clear image of yourself in a bright new mirror."

"Know in Part" versus "Know Fully"

The second part of verse 12 has also been interpreted as a contrast between the knowledge anyone has in this life and the knowledge we will have in heaven. This understanding would also support an eschatological interpretation of the *teleion*. That is, in this life all our knowledge is partial; only in heaven will we "know fully." Thus the partial gifts such as tongues must last until the second coming, for only then will we "know fully."

This view is based on a faulty view of the Greek words in verse 12b. Here there are two similar verbs for "to know": *ginosko* and *epiginosko*. The popular belief is that the latter word represents some special, intensified knowledge, such as one might have in heaven. This is why Bible versions translate it as "know *fully*." The "fully" is based solely on the prefix *epi-* on the front of *epiginosko;* there is no word in the Greek that means "fully."

The idea that there is such a contrast between *ginosko* and *epiginosko* is simply not true. The latter term does not necessarily carry any stronger meaning than the former. There is no warrant for translating it "know *fully*," in the sense of some kind of heavenly, quasi-divine knowledge. An examination of parallel places where these two words are used in the New Testament shows that they are used interchangeably. The article on "Knowledge" in the *New International Dictionary of New Testament Theology* mentions no distinction between these words. The major article on *ginosko* in Kittel's *Theological Dictionary of the New Testament* says they are used in the New Testament "interchangeably" and "with no difference in meaning."[5]

The object of our knowledge is not given; it is not important. The point is the contrast between two kinds or two levels of knowledge. Paul does not say we shall know *God* as fully as he knows us. Knowledge of God is not really the point. It is enough to conclude that with the more complete knowledge we have from the entire New Testament, we should know *ourselves* with more clarity, or know what we *ought* to be in a clearer way (see Jas 1:23-25). All thoughts of *full* knowledge in the sense of omniscience should be excluded altogether. Such knowledge is impossible for finite creatures, which we will always be, even in heaven.

Thus verse 12 is not speaking of a kind of end-times knowledge that will be ours only when we are glorified or only when we get to heaven or only when Jesus comes again. This verse is quite consistent with the meaning of *teleion* in verse 10 as the completed New Testament, which is a body of knowledge that is relatively clear and complete when compared with the fragments of knowledge given in the earliest days of the church via gifts of supernatural knowledge.

It stands firm that the best understanding of the *teleion* in 1 Corinthians 13:10 is that it refers to the completed New Testament. This confirms the fact that miraculous gifts ceased being passed along after the death of the apostles. The miraculous gifts filled a need in the absence of the written New Testament. Once the New Testament writings were in hand, this need ceased; thus the gifts ceased.

> **The best understanding of the *teleion* in 1 Corinthians 13:10 is that it refers to the completed New Testament.**

NOTES

1. "When" is the Greek word *hotan*. When used with a subjunctive verb, as is the case here, it means "when, but not before." Thus the tongues and other things must continue up to the time when the *teleion* comes.

2. This is based in part on verse 12, which will be discussed below.

3. The idea that good mirrors were not available in Bible times is a myth. See G. Kittel, "*ainigma*," in *Theological Dictionary of the New Testament*, ed. by Gerhard Kittel, trans. by G.W. Bromiley (Grand Rapids: Eerdmans, 1964), I:179, especially fn. 9. The whole article is relevant here (I:178-180).

4. We will of course see Jesus "face to face" in heaven, but that is not the point of this passage.

5. Rudolf Bultmann, "*ginosko*," *Theological Dictionary of the New Testament*, I:703.

> Publishers Note: The views and opinions expressed in the next chapter do not necessarily reflect the views and opinions of the staff and management of College Press Publishing Company, Inc.

~ 10 ~
THE HOLY SPIRIT AND DEMONIC COUNTERFEITS

In the preceding chapters I have presented biblical teaching to support the view that the Holy Spirit has not been giving miraculous spiritual gifts to Christians since late in the first century A.D. But there have been countless reports of miracles such as tongues and healings within Christian groups at different points during Christian history, especially since the early twentieth century. What shall we say about these claims? How can we explain them?

I once raised this question in a discussion with a teaching colleague who shares my cessationist convictions. His answer was, "We don't have to explain them. All we must do is teach and follow what the Bible says." This approach will not satisfy many, however; I know it does not satisfy me. Unless we can offer a plausible explanation for the allegedly miraculous phenomena, the case for cessationism is severely weakened. The point of this chapter is to offer such a plausible explanation.

Over the past 100 years, in America at least, the experience of miraculous gifts has arisen in three main stages. First came the rise of the Pentecostal movement. Its roots are usually traced to two events just after the turn of the twentieth century. One event was an experience of tongues in Topeka, Kansas, in 1901; the more influential event was the "Azusa Street revival" in Los Angeles in 1906. Pentecostalism involves specific Christian denominations, mostly having a kinship with the Wesleyan holiness movement. Such denominations include the Church of God in Christ, the

> The American experience of miraculous gifts has arisen in three main stages.

Church of God (Cleveland, TN), the Pentecostal Holiness Church, and the Assemblies of God.

The second stage was the rise of the charismatic movement in the early 1950s. Through the influence of the Full Gospel Business Men's Fellowship, Pentecostal doctrine and practice began to infiltrate mainline Christian groups such as the Episcopal, Lutheran, Presbyterian, and Catholic churches. The year 1960 is usually cited as the most identifiable starting point. This movement was at first called neo-Pentecostalism, but it was different enough that it soon took on its own name, i.e., the charismatic movement. The difference was not in doctrine or practice as such, but in the fact that Pentecostal doctrine and practice was now accepted in particular congregations and groups within most mainline denominations and in many independent congregations.

The third stage in the spread of miraculous practices on the American church scene is called the "signs and wonders" movement, or the "third wave" of the Holy Spirit. It can be traced to the late 1970s when John Wimber began the first Vineyard Christian Fellowship in Anaheim, California, with an emphasis on miraculous healing. This caught the attention of C. Peter Wagner, professor of missions and church growth at Fuller Theological Seminary in Pasadena. Wagner became convinced that miracles, especially divine healing, are a key component in church growth today. He and Wimber sparked renewed interest in miraculous gifts within evangelicalism.

The first two movements are linked together by their common belief that Pentecost introduced the baptism of the Holy Spirit as a distinct postconversion experience (a "second work" of grace), and that this baptism is evidenced by and results in miraculous phenomena, especially tongues. The three movements agree that all of the spiritual gifts named by Paul in 1 Corinthians 12, including the miraculous ones, are meant for the entire church age.

> Their common belief is that the "baptism of the Holy Spirit" is a "second work" of grace.

In the following discussion I will first in a general way explain the kinds of phenomena found within these movements; then I will outline possible explanations for them, defending one in particular.

"Miraculous" Phenomena

Regardless of how we explain it, we cannot ignore the abundant testimony claiming that miraculous events are occurring within Pentecostalism, the charismatic movement, and the signs and wonders movement. What sorts of phenomena are being reported? The anecdotal material is seemingly inexhaustible.

The most common phenomenon is speaking in tongues. In these circles this has always been important, usually being regarded as a sure sign that the much-coveted baptism of the Spirit has actually been received. Two kinds of tongues (called *glossalalia* from the Greek word for "tongue," *glossa*) are reported. One is the rapid utterance of nonlanguage, nondecipherable strings of syllables. The other is the rational speaking of unlearned foreign languages, similar to what happened on the Day of Pentecost (Acts 2:1-11).

> **Two kinds of tongues (glossalalia) are reported.**

There are abundant examples of the former (I have some on tape), but the latter are more dramatic. It is reported that a man named Dave Mangan prayed in tongues at a Pittsburgh gathering. A college student near him, a French major, was partially able to translate the prayer. She could not understand it all, though, and concluded it was an old French dialect. A week later a Frenchman named Paul was present and heard Dave again pray in tongues. The Frenchman said Dave *was* speaking French, but not modern French. He said Dave's pronunciation was flawless—but Dave had no background in the French language.[1]

A former Bible college classmate of mine had a Pentecostal experience and was later reported to have prayed in the (unlearned) Portuguese language while visiting Christians in Brazil. Pyle reports, "Missionaries from the Orient were persuaded, along with their Lancaster, Pennsylvania, pastor, to attend a tongues service. One woman poured forth a torrent of words

111

which the interpreter said was Chinese. Later the missionaries told the pastor that it was indeed Chinese."[2]

As this last incident shows, many also claim to have the gift of the interpretation of tongues.

There are also many reports of sick persons being healed, and not just by questionable and sometimes discredited television or "show business" healers. At Fuller Seminary, Peter Wagner and John Wimber actually cotaught a course on miracles and church growth, with healing demonstrations in the classroom. One of Wagner's healing specialities was leg-lengthening, i.e., causing the shorter leg to grow longer on a person whose legs were of uneven length.[3]

Gifts of supernatural knowledge and prophecy have also been reported. I know a missionary whose associates became charismatic and claimed to be receiving all sorts of prophetic messages by revelation from the Holy Spirit. I read some of them. A charismatic author reports that in the late 1970s he attended many meetings where "the pastor regularly revealed what someone [in the audience] was struggling with at the time, and he was invariably right."[4]

Numerous other kinds of miraculous phenomena have been reported. Certain Pentecostal groups have long practiced snake-handling, i.e., holding, caressing, and draping oneself with numerous poisonous snakes such as rattlers and copperheads, without protection. A popular practice in some circles is "slaying in the Spirit," or causing someone to lose consciousness and to collapse through a mere gesture or suggestion. Some groups have experienced uncontrollable fits of laughter, dubbed "holy laughter." A former Vineyard church in Toronto made news by claiming that in their services God was turning ordinary dental fillings into gold. They said God was simply keeping his promise in Psalm 81:10, "Open your mouth wide and I will fill it."[5]

Possible Explanations

How shall we respond to such reports and such claims? In this section I will simply outline the possible explanations, and I will affirm that no one explanation can apply to all of the phenomena.

Natural Explanations

First, we should note that the possible explanations can be divided into two kinds: natural and supernatural. Natural explanations are those that do not involve any divine or miraculous intervention. In such cases the phenomena are fully explainable in terms of natural processes.

One possible natural explanation is that the experiences in question are psychological in origin. The phenomena may be unusual, but may simply be the result of little-understood yet natural powers of the mind. For example, we are familiar with the concept of psychosomatic healing, where a physical ailment is the result of some kind of mental trauma. The ailment disappears when the trauma is neutralized.

For another example, some kinds of tongue-speaking could be triggered psychologically. In an effort to learn to speak in tongues, some have been told to begin repeating short phrases or nonsense syllables very fast, until the Holy Spirit takes over and bestows the genuine gift. I witnessed a friend's attempt to receive the gift of tongues. He knelt as family members laid their hands on his head and prayed in tongues, but nothing was happening. He was instructed to begin to babble until the Spirit took over. Still nothing happened. Kurt Koch reports that one person was told to repeat a short prayer, such as "Lord help me," five to eight hundred times. "Then your tongue and consciousness will get used to it and suddenly you will speak in 'tongues.'" Koch comments, "The Holy Spirit does not need repetitive exercises or any training of the subconsciousness."[6]

> Can many "charismatic" phenomena be explained by natural, psychological processes?

Another kind of natural explanation is that the alleged miraculous gifts are phony; they are being faked by unscrupulous ministers or attention-seekers. This certainly applies to some cases, especially in reference to certain big-name healers who have been

> **Can some "charismatic" phenomena be understood as the faked actions of attention-seekers?**

publicly exposed as frauds. Hugh Pyle tells of two women who kept interrupting a revival preacher with their tongue-speaking. One would stand and speak a message in tongues, and the other would give an interpretation. The minister arranged for a native Greek to memorize a short passage from the Greek New Testament, and to stand and quote it in a service attended by the two women. Once he had done so, one of the women enthusiastically stood and gave its "interpretation," which, of course, had no resemblance to the Bible text that was quoted. When the minister explained what had just happened, and read the relevant Scripture in English, "the 'tongues-speaking' women slunk away from the meeting and never returned."[7]

These are just two examples of possible natural explanations. It is likely that many of the allegedly miraculous phenomena can be explained thus. Things may happen through the power of our subconscious minds, and our inability to understand such workings may lead us to mistake them for miracles. Also, there are many naive and gullible people in the world, and many charlatans who know how to manipulate them and take advantage of them. However, in my judg-

> **It is clear that not all of the reported "miraculous" phenomena can be explained by natural means.**

ment it is clear that *not all* of the reported "miraculous" phenomena can be explained by natural means. One cannot conclude from a few obviously fake healings, e.g., that *all* alleged healings are phony.

Supernatural Explanations

If natural explanations cannot account for all allegedly miraculous phenomena, the only other possibility is a *supernatural* explanation. In such a case we would be acknowledging that the event in question is a true miracle. There are two possible supernatural explanations of true miracles. One is that they are from God. The Bible has many reports of miracles performed through the power of God. However, we have already ruled out this explanation for present-day events alleged to be miraculous. We have argued, on biblical grounds, that the Holy Spirit does not give miraculous gifts to Christians today. This does not mean that God is *unable* to work miracles today or unable to give miraculous gifts today. It simply means that he has chosen not to do so.

If someone says, "But I *saw* a genuine miracle," or "I was personally healed by a miracle, and in a church service no less," then I would ask that person to carefully read Matthew 7:21-23, where Jesus says:

> Not everyone who says to Me, "Lord, Lord," will enter the kingdom of heaven, but he who does the will of My Father who is in heaven will enter. Many will say to Me on that day, "Lord, Lord, did we not prophesy in Your name, and in Your name cast out demons, and in Your name perform many miracles?" And then I will declare to them, "I never knew you; DEPART FROM ME, YOU WHO PRACTICE LAWLESSNESS."

Here Jesus warns us that not every miraculous experience, including miraculous speaking (such as tongues), even when done in his own name, comes from God.

But if something miraculous is truly happening, and if it is not from God, how do we explain it? There is one other possible supernatural explanation for reports of miraculous events today. If such events are truly miraculous, they must be from Satan and his demonic spirits—even if they are happening in church circles. This will be explained in the next section.

The Occult Origin of "Christian" Miracles Today

I have reached the conclusion—not easily, I assure you—that all truly miraculous events that occur in Pentecostal, charismatic,

115

and third-wave circles have been and are being caused by demonic spirits working through unsuspecting people. This does not mean that those experiencing such demonic miracles or possessing demonic powers are deliberately allowing themselves to be used by the devil. They are basically victims of demonic deception. Many will think that I am going to a much too radical extreme here, and that this is an overly harsh judgment; but I see no other possibility.

The Reality of Demonic Miracles

Though some deny it, the Bible seems adequately clear about the reality of demonic miracles. In the text just quoted (Matt 7:21-23) Jesus implicitly affirms the existence of miracles that do not come from God. Pharaoh's magicians, Jannes and Jambres (2 Tim 3:8), were able to duplicate a limited number of Moses' miracles (Exod 7:11,22; 8:7,18). There is no reason to think this was anything less than demonic power at work.

In the New Testament Satanic miracles are linked especially with the end times (Matt 24:24; Rev 13:13; 16:14; 19:20). Speaking of a latter-day antichrist figure, Paul says that his "coming is in accord with the activity of Satan, with all power and signs and false wonders" (2 Thess 2:9). These are the three main words for miracles. "False wonders" does not mean phony miracles. The phrase is literally "wonders of falsehood," i.e., wonders or miracles performed in connection with falsehood. The old NIV is misleading: "counterfeit miracles, signs and wonders"; but the TNIV improves this to "signs and wonders that serve the lie."

> "Powers, signs, and false wonders" are the Bible's three main words for demonically originated miracles.

Our conclusion is that there is no biblical basis for denying the reality of demonic miracles.

The Reality of Demonic Miracles Today

Until the later 1960s, in America at least, it was easy to deny the reality of demonic miracles in postbiblical and modern times.

Unless one spent time on a mission field especially among animistic cultures, there was little overt demonic activity to be seen. In the late 1960s, however, encouraged by the widespread acceptance of relativism and pluralism, occultism and occult practices "came out of the closet," so to speak, and became culturally respectable. For about a decade an explosion of books on occultism appeared, both pro and con.

I confess that until this happened, I had no ready explanation for Pentecostal and charismatic miracles. But the flood of incontrovertible evidence being presented about the reality of occult supernatural practices opened up a new possible explanation. It became very clear that demonic miracles have been and are now occurring in pagan and Satanic circles the world over. Such were simply not openly practiced and openly examined until the late 1960s and following.

I began my career as a seminary professor in 1967, just as this was beginning to happen. Thus from the beginning I felt compelled to prepare and teach courses both on demonism and on occultism. I have learned that all the forms of occultism condemned by the Bible are widespread today. This includes occult or demonic *knowledge* of all sorts: ESP, divination, future-telling, ouija boards, and tongue-speaking in unlearned human languages. Anyone who doubts the reality of supernatural knowledge from demonic sources today should study carefully the life and work of Edgar Cayce.[8]

> The forms of occultism condemned by the Bible are widespread today, including occult or demonic knowledge of all sorts.

I have also become convinced of the reality of occult or demonic *power* today, involving true miracles. These occur in the context of witchcraft or sorcery, and sometimes involve miraculous healings. Anyone who doubts such possibilities should study the life of the Brazilian healer, Arigo, called "the surgeon of the rusty knife."[9]

The third category of the occult, also prohibited in the Bible, is *spiritism*, or the supposed communication with the spirits of the dead. Both supernatural knowledge and miraculous events take place in this context. The Christian minister Ben Alexander, a former spiritist, testifies to their reality. He also confirms the fact that the spirits with which spiritists communicate are demons, not the souls of dead people.[10]

The sobering truth is this: the same phenomena that occur in Pentecostal and charismatic circles also occur in pagan and demonic circles. This includes speaking in tongues and miraculous healing. This in itself would not imply that the charismatic phenomena are demonic in origin, of course. But in view of the reasons given in chapters 8 and 9 for denying that the Holy Spirit is giving miraculous powers today, it seems probable that demonic powers are the true source of any truly miraculous or supernatural activity within these Christian circles.

> I find it impossible to deny that demonic powers can work and are working in Christian circles.

The Reality of Demonic Miracles within Christian Circles

This, of course, is the most difficult aspect of the view I am proposing. How can we possibly think that demonic powers could have a foothold within Christians themselves and within the very sphere of the church? Before dismissing such a possibility out of hand, one should read again Jesus' words in Matthew 7:21-23. Those who were performing the alien miracles were doing so *in Jesus' name.*

Earlier in this chapter I mentioned Hugh Pyle's report of missionaries who attended a tongues service in a Lancaster, Pennsylvania, church and heard someone speak in a tongue identified as Chinese. Here is the rest of the story: "Later the missionaries told the pastor that it was indeed Chinese—the most indescribable filth and profanity that could be phrased in the Chinese language!"[11] Without a doubt a demonic spirit was the source of that "tongue."

Many deliverance ministers in recent times have persuaded tongue-speakers to submit to an examination known as "testing tongues." While the subject is calmly speaking in tongues, the tester addresses questions directly to the spirit who is the source of the tongue, who answers in English through the subject's vocal apparatus. I have a tape recording of one such test, in which Ernest Rockstadt, a deliverance ministry pioneer, questions such a spirit. Part of it goes like this:

Rockstadt: "Do you love the blood of Jesus?" Spirit: "NO."

"Do you confess Jesus has come in the flesh?" "NO."

"Is Jesus Christ your Lord?" "NO."

"Is Satan your Lord?" "YES."

"Are you defeated through the cross?" "YES."

"What is your opinion of the blood of the Lord Jesus?" "I HATE IT."

"Is the blood of Jesus holy?" "YES."

"Do you love Him?" "NO."

"Why don't you love him? "HE DOESN'T LOVE ME."

"Who have you been praying to?" "THE DEVIL."

"What have you been saying to him? "I LOVE THE DEVIL."

Many other counselors have had similar experiences.[12]

For such reasons I find it impossible to deny that demonic powers can work and are working in Christian circles. It is the only consistent explanation of what is going on in the Pentecostal, charismatic, and third-wave movements today.

Many questions and objections may be raised, of course. One is whether it is possible for demonic power to be at work in the life of a God-fearing person. The answer is definitely yes. One may refer again to the life of Edgar Cayce, who began his journey into occultism as a pious, Bible-believing member of a Christian church.

Another question is why would Satan empower works that are good and beneficial to mankind, such as healings? The answer is that this helps him all the more to deceive those who "did not receive the love of the truth" (2 Thess 2:10). A possible Satanic goal is a new ecumenical movement based solely upon experience, with a diminished place for sound doctrine.

> A possible Satanic goal is a church focused on experience, with a diminished place for sound doctrine.

119

Finally, is there any possibility that anyone who affirms that modern tongues and such are demonic is guilty of the unpardonable sin, or blasphemy against the Holy Spirit? Certainly not, if the suggestion is true—which I believe it is. In any case, this is not at all parallel to the kind of sin Jesus calls blasphemy against the Spirit in Matthew 12:22-32. For a good discussion of the unpardonable sin see W. Carl Ketcherside, *Heaven Help Us (The Holy Spirit in Your Life)* (Cincinnati: Standard, 1974) ch. 7, "What Is the Sin against the Spirit?"

Conclusion

In view of the above conclusions, how should Christians today respond to the false Pentecostal or charismatic phenomena and experiences within Christendom?

First, *do not seek such gifts!* Doing so makes one vulnerable to becoming demonized.

Second, pray for those caught up in these entanglements, and try to rescue them. Try to confront them with Matthew 7:21-23 and with other truths set forth here. Always do this in a spirit of love. Remember, these folks are victims, not villains.

Third (this is especially for church leaders), do not allow your congregation to be damaged by such activity. Do not allow a small group of charismatics to exert influence over others and lead them astray. Do not sit by passively while some are practicing these "gifts," even if they are not perceived as a threat to the church as a whole. They are putting themselves in jeopardy.

Fourth (also for leaders), make sure your congregation is educated about these matters before problems arise.

NOTES

1. Kevin and Dorothy Ranaghan, *Catholic Pentecostals* (Paramus, NJ: Paulist Press, 1969), 177.
2. Hugh F. Pyle, *Truth about Tongues* (Denver: Accent Books, 1976), 13.

120

3. Ken Sarles, "An Appraisal of the Signs and Wonders Movement," *Bibliotheca Sacra* (January–March 1988), 62-63.

4. Craig Keener, *3 Crucial Questions about the Holy Spirit* (Grand Rapids: Baker, 1996), 113.

5. James Beverley, "Dental Miracle Reports Draw Criticism," *Christianity Today* (5/29/99), 17.

6. Kurt Koch, *The Strife of Tongues* (Grand Rapids: Kregel, 1971), 24.

7. Pyle, *Truth about Tongues*, 76-77.

8. See Gary North, *Unholy Spirits: Occultism and New Age Humanism* (Ft. Worth: Dominion Press, 1986), 193-225.

9. See John G. Fuller, *Arigo: Surgeon of the Rusty Knife* (New York: Pocket Books, 1975).

10. See Ben Alexander, *Out from Darkness* (Joplin, MO: College Press, 1985).

11. Pyle, *Truth about Tongues*, 13.

12. See Grayson Ensign and Edward Howe, *Counseling and Demonization* (Amarillo, TX: Recovery Publications, 1989), Appendix J, 294-300, "Speaking in Tongues and the Testing of Tongues."

AFTERWORD

Living in a physical world in material bodies, even Christians are constantly vulnerable to the error of materialism. Theoretically we believe in the existence of spiritual realities—God, angels, demons, our own souls. But on a practical level we often live as if none of these spiritual realities are really *real*. We limit our conscious lives to what can be perceived through our five senses—all of which are physical.

Even in our relation to God, the physical often takes priority. In prayer, for example, we focus on physical blessings and needs. In group prayer sessions, when prayer requests are solicited, usually the great majority of such requests are for some kind of physical healing of physical ailments.

It is certainly not wrong to be fully aware of and thankful for this physical creation, and it is quite appropriate to petition and to thank God for our physical well-being. However, we must always resist the temptation to *limit* our concerns to the material aspects of reality. My prayer is that those who have studied this little book about the Holy Spirit will thereby have a heightened sensitivity to the *spiritual* presence and *spiritual* work of God in our lives.

The Holy Spirit is real; he is one of the three persons who are the one true and living God. He is literally present in the lives and bodies of those who have obeyed the gospel (Acts 2:38; 5:32; 1 Cor 6:19). Our own spirits have been changed by his presence: he has regenerated and renewed us (Titus 3:5); he has raised us up from spiritual death. He now works within us to make us holy as he is holy (Phil 2:13; 1 Pet 1:15-16). He is the source of our spiritual strength to fight temptation and overcome sin (Rom 8:13; Eph 3:16).

This is not something we will discover through any of our five senses. We do not literally see the Holy Spirit enter our bodies in our baptism; we do not literally feel him moving around under our skin. In this matter, as in many others, "we walk by faith, not by sight" (2 Cor 5:7). We believe these things are true because we believe in the utter truthfulness of the Bible.

Having, then, accepted these spiritual realities on faith, let us indeed *walk* by this faith. Let us truly seek the indwelling Spirit's power to overcome whatever sin still plagues us. Let us place our hand in his, and allow him to lead us in paths of righteousness. Let us gladly use the gifts with which he has equipped us, to do our part in building up the body of Christ.

How can we do these things? How can we dare to be spiritual in such a physical world? I leave you with a challenge. In order to heighten our awareness of the Spirit's reality in our lives, I challenge everyone (including myself) to make an effort to *acknowledge* the Holy Spirit's presence more and more every day. One way this can be done is by making a list of Bible passages that speak about the Holy Spirit, and reading at least one of them every day. It can be done by mentioning the Spirit more in our daily prayers, e.g., by thanking God for his presence and his working within us, or by wording a petition based on texts such as Romans 8:13 and Ephesians 3:16. Writing out the Scriptures and prayers by hand can serve to sharpen our awareness of the Spirit even further.

If we make an effort to *acknowledge* the Holy Spirit's presence more and more every day, then perhaps we will be on our way to fulfilling what Paul had in mind for us when he gave us this exhortation, "Be filled with the Spirit" (Eph 5:18).

STUDY GUIDE

Chapter 1: Who Is the Holy Spirit

1. Why is it important that we understand the Holy Spirit to be a "person" instead of simply an "active force"? (pp. 7-8)

2. Jesus calls the Holy Spirit "another helper" in John 14:16. Discuss the consolation we share as Christians, knowing that the Holy Spirit is a personal "comforter." (pp. 9-10)

3. Dr. Cottrell lists five traits of personhood the Scriptures attribute to the Holy Spirit. How can each of these aid us both in our understanding of God and in our walk with the Lord? (pp. 12-13)

4. The Bible teaches that God is one in essence but exists eternally in three distinct persons. How does the false teaching of "modalism" differ from the biblical teaching of the Trinity? (pp. 13-15)

5. Why do you think that "blasphemy against the Holy Spirit" is such a severe sin in Jesus' teaching (Matt 12:32; Luke 12:10)? (pp. 15-16)

6. Have you ever known someone to refer to the Holy Spirit as an "it"? Why is this always inappropriate? (pp. 16-17)

Chapter 2: The Holy Spirit and the Bible

1. What are the two main "works" of the Holy Spirit? Why is it important that we make a distinction between these works? (p. 19)

2. Dr. Cottrell draws a distinction between the concepts of "revelation" and "inspiration." How are these concepts different? How are they related? (pp. 20-21)

3. Both the Old and New Testaments often equate the words of Scripture with the voice of God's Holy Spirit. How should this affect our approach to the study of the Bible? (pp. 21-23)

4. Discuss some of the ways the Holy Spirit inspired the authors of Scripture. What does this teach us about the way the Holy Spirit works? (pp. 23-24)

5. Discuss Dr. Cottrell's three objections to the doctrine of illumination. Why is the unbiblical doctrine of illumination a dangerous teaching? How is the spiritual gift of wisdom different from the doctrine of illumination? (pp. 25-29)

Chapter 3: The Holy Spirit and the New Age

1. Dr. Cottrell discusses three distinct works of the Holy Spirit in the life of both the church and individual Christians: 1) miraculous power, 2) ministering power, and 3) moral power. Do you agree with these categories? Why or why not? (p. 31)

2. In the prophecies of the coming of a "new era of the Spirit," the imagery of water is often used to describe the work of the Holy Spirit. Discuss the uses of this imagery. (pp. 33-34)

3. What was the purpose of the miracles associated with the Day of Pentecost in Acts 2? (pp. 36-38)

4. What is the difference between the Holy Spirit "coming upon" an individual and the Holy Spirit "indwelling" an individual? (pp. 38-39)

5. Why are those who see miracles as the "purpose" of the events surrounding Pentecost missing the point? (p. 40)

Chapter 4: The Holy Spirit and the Sinner

1. How does the Holy Spirit generate faith and repentance in the heart of a sinner? (pp. 42-43)

2. Describe a time in your life when the Holy Spirit worked on your heart through the written Word of God.

3. Dr. Cottrell discusses how the Holy Spirit works "indirectly" on the heart through the Word of God. How does the Holy Spirit work "directly" on our hearts? Can you think of a time when the Holy Spirit worked directly on your own heart? (pp. 45-47)

4. Can people resist both the indirect and direct work of the Holy Spirit upon their hearts? Can you think of a time when you resisted the Spirit's prompting upon your heart?

5. Why is the Calvinist view of the work of the Holy Spirit upon the heart of a sinner in contradiction with both Scripture and common sense? (pp. 49-50)

Chapter 5: The Holy Spirit and Conversion

1. How does Dr. Cottrell define the term "conversion"? (p. 51)

2. Why is it so important to understand "regeneration" as the work of the Holy Spirit? (pp. 53-55)

3. Read Romans 6:1-11, Colossians 2:12, and Titus 3:5. Discuss how these passages teach that baptism seems to be the normal time when God promises regeneration? (pp. 55-56)

4. Discuss the difference between baptism being the "time" of regeneration as opposed to it being the "cause" of regeneration. (pp. 56-57)

5. Do you agree with Dr. Cottrell's conclusion that "water baptism" and "Spirit baptism" are the same thing? Discuss your reasons. (pp. 58-59)

Chapter 6: The Holy Spirit and Sanctification

1. Discuss the images the Bible uses to describe the indwelling presence of the Holy Spirit in the life of the Christian. (pp. 62-63)

2. Why is it dangerous to base our assurance of the Spirit's presence on a "feeling"? (p. 63)

3. Discuss the difference between "initial" sanctification and "progressive" sanctification. (pp. 64-65)

4. How does the Holy Spirit sanctify us in knowledge? (p. 66)

5. How does the Holy Spirit sanctify us in power? (pp. 66-68)

6. Dr. Cottrell maintains that the leading of the Spirit does not involve knowledge (through subjective experience), but rather involves an "inward empowerment of the will." What does this look like in the life of someone being "led by the Spirit"? (p. 68)

7. Review Dr. Cottrell's eightfold path to spiritual empowerment. Discuss how you have experienced this in your own life. (pp. 70-71)

Chapter 7: The Holy Spirit and Spiritual Gifts

1. Why is it a mistake to equate "natural gifts" with "spiritual gifts"? (pp. 73-75)

2. Dr. Cottrell maintains that a spiritual gift is usually associated with a call to a specific task, office, or role (p. 75). He supports this with a considerable amount of scriptural evidence (pp. 75-79). Do you agree or disagree? Why or why not?

3. What is the purpose of spiritual gifts? How does the "body" metaphor illustrate this purpose? (pp. 79-80)

4. Some spiritual gifts are "temporary." Why are these gifts not intended to be present in every age of the church? (pp. 81-82)

5. Some spiritual gifts are "permanent." Why are these gifts intended to be present in every age of the church? (pp. 82-83)

Chapter 8: The Holy Spirit and Miracles Today

1. Why is it biblically inaccurate to call a natural event (such as a beautiful sunrise or the birth of a baby) a "miracle"? (p. 86)

2. Dr. Cottrell discusses three supernatural events: 1) special providence, 2) supernatural spiritual events, and 3) miracles. Discuss how these display God's work in the world. Discuss how they are similar and yet distinctively different. (pp. 87-88)

3. What is the narrow biblical definition of a miracle? (p. 88)

4. What are the three words used in the New Testament for the concept of a miracle? Which one best describes the purpose of a miracle? Why? (pp. 89-90)

5. In the New Testament era, what was the connection between the "laying on of Apostles' hands" and the ability to perform miracles? (pp. 91-92)

6. Summarize the arguments for those who believe that "miraculous gifts" continue today. What problems can be associated with these views? (pp. 92-95)

Chapter 9: The Holy Spirit and 1 Corinthians 13:8-13

1. Summarize the context of 1 Corinthians 12–14. (pp. 98-99)

2. How are permanent Christian traits (such as faith, hope, and love) contrasted with temporary gifts (such as prophecy, knowledge, and tongues) in 1 Corinthians 13:8-13? (pp. 99-100)

3. Dr. Cottrell defines the "perfect" in 1 Corinthians 13:10 as the "completed New Testament." Discuss his arguments. What are their strengths? Could there be any possible weaknesses? (pp. 100-104)

4. What potential problem(s) does Dr. Cottrell's interpretation of 1 Corinthians 13 help Christians to avoid? Are there any drawbacks to such an interpretation?

Chapter 10: The Holy Spirit and Demonic Counterfeits

1. Historically, there are three main stages of the spread of the "miraculous gifts movement" over the past 100 years. List them and discuss your knowledge or association with any of them. (pp. 109-110)

2. Discuss your reactions to the miraculous stories shared by Dr. Cottrell. (pp. 111-112)

3. What are some of the possible "natural" explanations to such (allegedly) miraculous experiences? (pp. 113-114)

4. What are some of the possible "supernatural" explanations of such (allegedly) miraculous experiences? (pp. 114-116)

5. Dr. Cottrell has reluctantly concluded that all true modern-day miracles occurring in Pentecostal/charismatic/third wave circles are demonic in origin (pp. 115-120). Do you agree or disagree with his argument and conclusion? Why or why not?

6. What is the author's recommended Christian response to the Pentecostal/charismatic phenomenon? (p. 120)

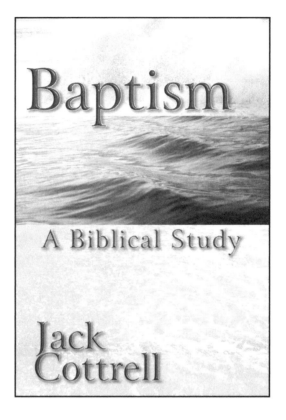

Baptism: A Biblical Study
Jack Cottrell

In this classic work, Dr. Cottrell guides you through every New Testament text that deals with baptism. It is a thorough, yet highly readable, study that provides a firm understanding of the New Testament teaching concerning this important doctrinal issue.

170 pages, softcover, HSB-341-9, $10.99

College Press Publishing
1-800-289-3300 • www.collegepress.com

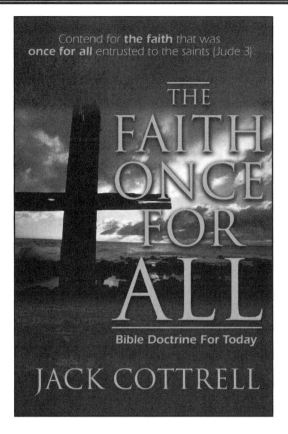